ARTS = EDUCATION

Connecting Learning Communities in Los Angeles

ARTS = EDUCATION

Connecting Learning Communities in Los Angeles

Amy Shimshon-Santo, Editor

Published by the Center for Learning Through Arts and Technology
University of California, Irvine

Distributed in association with University of California Press
Berkeley, Los Angeles, London

2010

Published by the Center for Learning Through Arts and Technology
University of California, Irvine

Distributed in association with University of California Press
Berkeley, Los Angeles, London

Cover Art: Paul Soady & Chris Davies
Back Cover Image: Willem Henri Lucas

Library of Congress Control Number: 2010933319

ISBN: 9780982873502

Manufactured in the United States of America

10 9 8 7 6 5 4 3 2 1

The paper used in this publication meets the minimum requirements of
ANSI/NISO Z39.48-1992 (R1997) [Permanence of Paper]

Dedication

This book is dedicated to the diligent teaching artists, determined youth and families, generous guiding teachers, munificent school and university administrators, and inventive community organizations that brought each creative collaboration to life. Together we created opportunities to risk, plant, weed, and cultivate an abundant garden of fruitful learning experiences. Life lessons never stopped sprouting up. The participants honored herein unflinchingly confronted the inertia and complacency that all too often silence minds, classrooms, school, and cities from knowing how creativity brightens transformative teaching.

Gratitude

The content of this book is the result of an extensive process of action and reflection, but it is also a creation unto itself. Special thanks are due to the following individuals who helped make this new edition a reality: Liane Brouillette, Maureen Burns, Laura Cerruti, Barbara Cohen, Kori Hamilton, Libero Dizinno, Paul Soady, Chris Davies, and Henri Lucas. Each drop of their guidance or support was somehow crucial along the way to bring this book into existence. Paul Soady's keen eyes, artful pencil markings, and generous cups of tea provided the compass that guided me through the uncharted territory of manuscript design.

May I be a bridge
a boat
and a ship
for all who wish to cross (the water)

May I be an island
for those who seek one
and a lamp
for those desiring light

May I be a bed
for all who wish to rest...

May I be a wish fulfilling tree.

- SHANTIDEVA (8th Century)

CONTENTS

CORRELATE

FOREWORD

We are born creative, an essential aspect of our being as humans. Animals may have embedded instincts and behavior, but we have the capacity to connect our soul to our mind to our heart, and our ability to do so comes from our creativity. Through such a path, we express ourselves in ways that makes something where nothing was there before: we make Art, and as a group, we create our mutual culture.

To be denied access to our own creativity, whether through purposeful caprice or willful neglect, is to deny a fundamental human function and expression that leaves us in a vacuum of self understanding, stunting us as individuals in a society, or muting us as a group developing an identity.

In recent years, the realization of how Art and culture are fundamental to a healthy society, are cornerstones of a fulfilled education, and are proven assets to local economies, has become clearly measured and irrefutable. Yet the contradiction to these truths has been a sustained pattern of diminishing support and resources, which foster these very attributes of Art and culture.

Arts education is posited as a worthy pursuit, but only as an adjunct to core study, and subject to elimination in times of dire economic cutbacks. Formal public school systems have already demonstrated that they do not regard the Arts as a vital strand of a standard education. Legions of professional educators in public office or leadership will protest and decry this statement as unjust, but few will act to insure that the Arts are included in the school systems they are sworn to oversee.

In smaller arenas, such as private or charter schools in well financed communities where resources are adequate, if not plentiful, Arts training and learning is still part of the curriculum, and those students benefit from the skill development and nurturing of creativity which come from the Arts. Thus, the issues of access or socio-economic restrictions become amplified and agitated by the distinction of wealth and class.

Community based after-school programs, as well as university based Arts program partnerships, become all the more critical in these times, as valuable access and opportunity for participation in the Arts for youth and students who otherwise have no other outlets. Once again, such partnerships are imperiled by ever dwindling resources, despite the effort of some honorable foundations and private sponsors, with the potential loss of a unique learning environment for all parties and interests.

Indeed, many of those successful programs are witnessing an ever increasing challenge of maintaining operations commensurate with a growing population of youth and students in communities who are also demonstrating an increasing demand for Arts and culture in the absence and failure of local school systems.

Service to need is not the only benefit that comes from such partnerships and Arts programs. The endeavor of the community and university working in tandem to provide Arts and cultural experiences yields a plethora of new paradigms for Arts learning that is beneficial to both entities. Successful programs will recognize the depth of the mutual value which both the community and university offer, in their goals to create new and exciting opportunities. What the community has to offer is no less important than what the university has to give, and the community offers the pathway for the university to not only extend the learning environment, but to integrate itself within the population it aspires to serve. The program thus becomes the synapse that connects the learning community with the larger community, nurturing the goals, objectives and needs of all parties.

This working book annotates several models of success of not only community-based programs, but of arts based learning, and in turn, of valuable cultural arts based community building. What becomes evident is that there are methodologies and projects that work, always taking into account the organic elements of the different settings. Yet, the value of experience, lessons learned, wisdom distilled, and the success of the valiant efforts put forth by the partners, programs, and teachers are documented here, not as a template to be reproduced, but as inspiration and proof that Arts = education and serves the very creativity of our state of being human.

- TOMAS J. BENITEZ, Commissioner
Los Angeles County Arts Commission

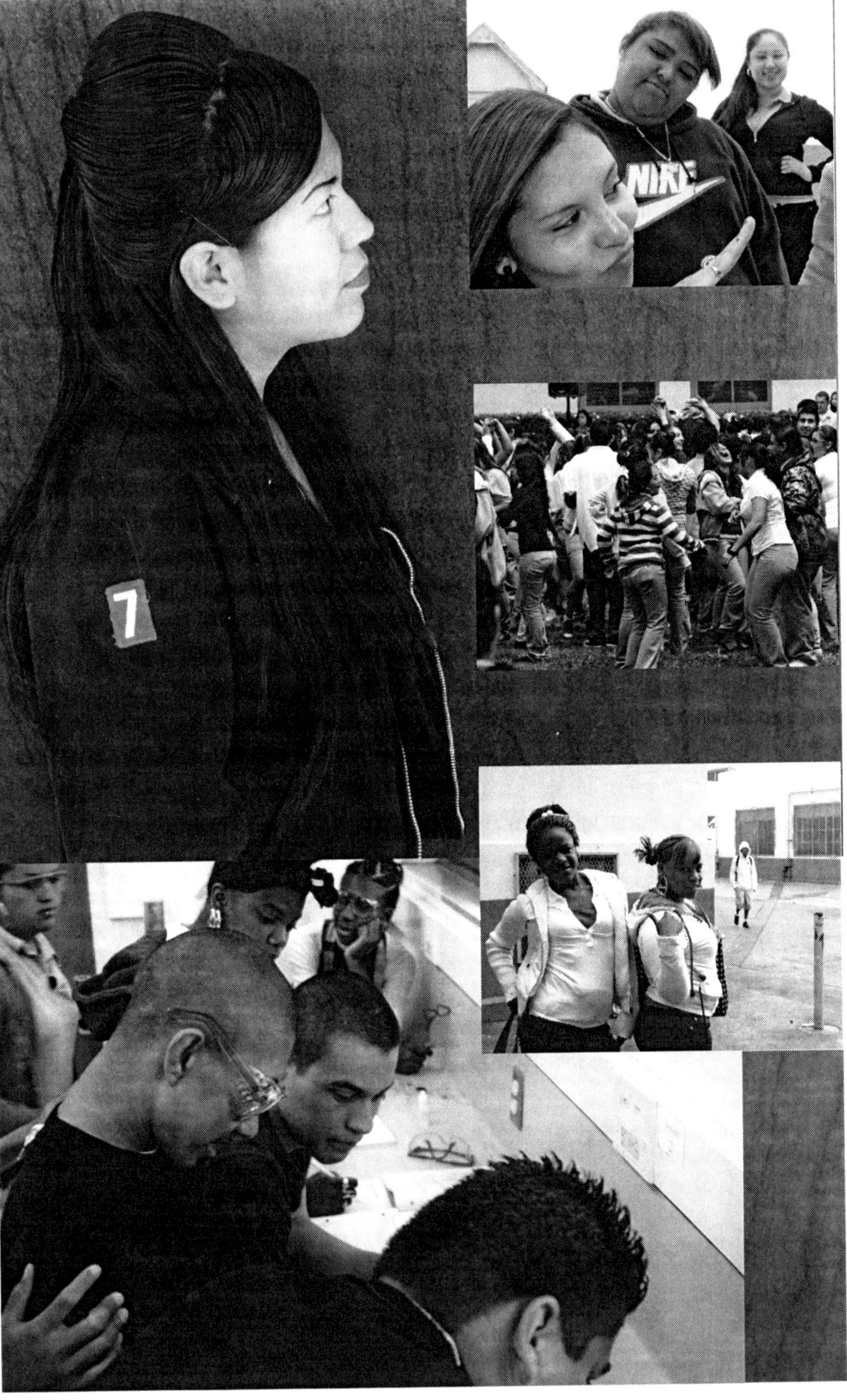

INTRODUCTION

Arts educators have the power to prepare students in ways that standard schooling often overlooks. The greatest finding from this study has been the positive impact that Arts education clearly has on one's sense of personal value and peer relationships. A positive sense of self-efficacy and community value are the basic building blocks for courageous learning, life fulfillment, and social change.

Two years before the Los Angeles uprising in 1992, I started to think of myself not only as a dancer and performer, but, also, as an arts educator. By that time, I had already studied dance in and outside of the university, performed, choreographed, toured, and taught dance to others. However, teaching the arts in public schools felt qualitatively different. The experience ignited a vital awareness of important roles for artists as educators and the arts to public schooling.

Developing the skills I needed to teach did not come easily. When I was an undergraduate dance major at the University of California, Santa Cruz, classes were not offered in arts education. As the field of arts education grew, the non-profit sector and the state arts agencies provided the lion's share of teacher preparation in the arts, and universities remained largely outside of the loop. As a result, I remember struggling terribly as I led my first sequential dance residency to children at the 112th Street School in South Los Angeles for the Los Angeles County Music Center's Education Division. Little by little, over the next twenty years, I became a capable arts educator and wound up teaching and performing not only in hundreds of schools throughout the city, but also in the country and abroad.

I witnessed the field of arts education transform completely, and I changed along with it. It was the recognition of a need for rigorous teacher preparation for artists, a passion for teaching and learning through the arts, and a commitment to social justice that inspired me to take action. I accepted the challenge graciously offered to me by UCLA's School of the Arts and Architecture, to direct the school's ArtsBridge program, prepare arts educators in dance, world music, design|media arts, architecture, and visual art, and to cultivate community partnerships with inner city schools. Community partnerships in the arts connected University of California students and faculty with primary and secondary teachers, students, and parents in South and Central Los Angeles schools. Together, we reached across what is called the educational "pipeline," which all too often breaks down between inner city schools and institutions of higher learning.

This book grew out of that experience. It compiles distinct voices that paint a broad based picture of involvement and impact. Readers will hear from novice arts educators, experienced classroom teachers, youth, parents, and school administrators as they discuss their arts education experiences. The book is structured into five sections clustered around the metaphors of reach, process, translate, correlate, and assess. I have composed section overviews to orient readers to each selection of essays and student work samples. Appendices at the end of the book will be helpful to aspiring arts educators.

The *Reach* section introduces the book and paints the bigger picture, framing the bigger picture of the university and school partnerships discussed in the subsequent sections. Leah Bass-Bayliss and Kori Hamilton, who both served as school site coordinators at their secondary schools, discuss the challenges and benefits of building a partnership between schools and the university.

The *Process* section highlights critical essays and student work samples from novice arts educators. These essays capture the pivotal moment when arts educators - equipped with creative experience, clear intentions for teaching and learning, and meticulously scaffolded lesson plans - are confronted by real, live students, each demanding her own way into the material. The act of beginning requires a leap of faith where theory weds practice. Quality educators both teach and learn from their students as they attempt to make the content accessible to diverse learners. Individual learning benefits from a supportive community with high expectations. Teachers also benefit from professional learning communities. Similarly, students learn from teachers as well as from their families and their own peers.

The *Translate* section includes essays about the theme of translation. Los Angeles is a global city where hundreds of different languages are spoken in the public schools. In addition to linguistic differences, a kind of cultural translation is required of many students as they journey from home to school and back again. This same translation and adaptation is required when moving back and forth between the university and the schools. Learning conditions vary widely across the city. Inner city schools and the university are distinctly populated and differently equipped in terms of resources. We captured this dynamic through a visual storytelling project supported by Iris Schneider, former *Los Angeles Times* photo editor, and by Canon Cameras. In addition to visual storytelling about places of study, essays analyzing how arts education can validate bilingual and polylingual learning and promote language acquisition take center stage in this section.

The *Correlate* section compiles essays from novice arts educators who were required in my courses to analyze what they did and what they learned from teaching. These essays emphasize arts integration teaching methods. Arts integration is teaching and learning that ties the arts curriculum to other subject area. For example, it was common for participants to develop curricula linking art to science, literature to theater, dance to health, and architecture to social studies. For many schools that are uneasy providing Arts education instruction for their students, Arts integration is a useful alternative for imbuing creativity into the mandated curriculum matrix.

Each year, we made time to gather participants (including children, teens, and adults) to share project processes and production. Gathering provided an important outlet to build community, share work, and assess our actions. The final section, *Assess*, includes highlights from these gatherings including work samples as well as student and teacher reflections. Excerpts from these phenomenal gatherings are also available in video form on YouTube.

This book concludes with lessons learned and final evaluations. The question is asked, "Did we meet our aims?" The rich anecdotal, analytical, and artistic work that constitutes the body of this book is supported by concrete statistical analysis of learning outcomes for youth and student teachers. Talented evaluator Mark Hansen, of SRM Evaluation, inspired us to develop logic models, as well as pre and post survey instruments, which allowed us to better quantify our stated and real progress over time. The data was used to improve the program and to share with the field. "Lessons Learned" offers scientifically grounded quantitative analysis of program impact verifying the transformations that took place.

It was a remarkable challenge to work and innovate alongside such committed youth, educators, and administrators who shared the goals of inspiring creative achievement and college preparation for under-resourced schools, preparing a new generation of arts educators for work in urban spaces and cultivating mutually beneficial community partnerships between inner city schools and the university. We hope that participants feel their important efforts are appropriately honored in this compendium, and that readers learn from the eclectic and revealing reflections herein.

Creativity is crucial to learning. There is a place for arts education in every public school and every university where educators are being prepared. Looking back on this amazing journey, I see that it was the resilient power of the imagination and the real human connections of collaboration and friendship developed among participants that wove the rope and skillful knotting required to build bridges of opportunity and growth. The vital learning experiences we shared can now reach and inspire a broader circle of students, teachers, artists, and administrators through the publication and reading of this book.

LEAP OF FAITH:
ONE JOURNEY IN EDUCATION THROUGH THE ARTS

Kori Hamilton

Theater and performance have always occupied a significant space in my life. Beginning with dance at four years old, I was involved with the Arts all the way through college, both through dance and stage performance. The Arts have always seemed like a necessary and important component to my learning and development, which is why the degree that I hold from Georgetown University is English with a minor in Theatre. My English background and some incredible experiences working with youth in Washington, D.C. initially drew me into the field of education.

The first year of teaching always comes with a learning curve, but I was not prepared for its steepness. Being a first year teacher at a middle school in Watts, California, a community and a school that had a reputation of being extremely challenging, forced me to reevaluate my skill level. Feeling ill-equipped to provide the students the type of education that they deserved, I decided to return to school and enroll in a teacher preparation program at UCLA to better develop my teaching skills. That is where I was able to really develop my teaching philosophy and begin to make connections between theory and practice.

Coming from a background of English and Art I recognized a natural connection between the two, but my graduate program helped me to explore the theoretical correlations as well. There were a few theorists whose concepts resonated with me and made my work begin to have more significant meaning. Pierre Bourdieu developed a concept that examines different kinds of capital: social, cultural, and economic. Cultural capital is made up of embodied capital, which refers to speech, mannerisms, interests or culture. The other aspect of cultural capital is academic capital, which is simply related to level and type of education. In "Distinction: A Social Critique of the Judgement of Taste," Bourdieu states that "All cultural practices and preferences in literature, painting or music are closely linked to educational level and secondarily to social origin". This illustrates that preferences in literature and the Arts are indicators of social and educational status. This notion informs my practice by explicitly revealing the importance of exposure and interaction with literature and the Arts. Bourdieu offers the piece of theory that fully embodies my two passions, English literature and the Arts.

The other theorists that my teaching and education philosophy were born from provide a frame for the necessity and urgency of creating space that gives students access to higher levels of cultural capital. Paolo Freire, in *Pedagogy of the Oppressed*, presents the banking model as a form of educating oppressed groups. According to Freire, "The capability of banking education to minimize or annul the students' creative power and to stimulate their credulity serves the interests of the oppressors". In other words, the banking model benefits those who have the highest levels of capital in all forms, also known at the oppressors. The other issue with banking information is "The more students work at storing the deposits entrusted to them, the less they develop the critical consciousness which would result from their intervention in the world as transformers of that world". I wanted to develop transformers of the world and not continue to maintain the status quo.

Gloria Ladson-Billings and W.E.B. DuBois close out my theoretical foundation. Ladson-Billings' *Toward a Critical Race Theory of Education* conveys practical concepts that just make sense, while reminding me that my decision to pursue a Master's degree, and currently a doctorate, is part of the necessary process to make significant and meaningful strides in education. She says "Intellectual property must be under girded by 'real' property, that is, science labs, computers, and other state-of-the-art technologies, appropriately certified and prepared teachers". Prepared teachers are essential to elevating the intellectual property of students; teachers are the real property that support and develop the intellectual property. DuBois also discusses the role of teachers as agents of change. He proposes that " '[Teachers] must also, so far as possible, be broad minded, cultured men and women, to scatter civilization among people whose ignorance was not simply of letters, but of life itself." Teachers must be well read, versed and experienced in order to take the students beyond the text and into the world.

As I began to gain a greater understanding of my work and its importance, I knew that I had to follow my middle school students to high school, so I could try to fill in some of that gaps that I left them with in middle school. When I first walked onto Jordan's campus, I was met with many hugs and questions. The most consistent question was "Ms. Hamilton, what are you doing here?" My response was always some variation of "I am checking on you, of course." That first year at Jordan, I met Dr. Amy Shimshon-Santo who was working with Dana Escalante, the lead teacher of the performing and visual arts Small Learning Community (SLC). They were trying to forge a partnership between the performing and visual arts SLC and the UCLA School of the Arts and Architecture's ArtsBridge program. It took an entire year for the partnership to begin to have some footing and for supports, particularly at the school site, to be put in place. Dana, as the lead teacher of a newly formed SLC, was so flooded administratively, instructionally, and creatively with responsibilities that I took the role of facilitating the partnership. We worked very closely and intensely the second year to make sure that a foundation of support was being laid. There my journey as a guiding teacher, and school coordinator for the partnership, began.

Being a Guiding Teacher to an ArtsBridge Scholar was one of the most rewarding experiences anyone can have as an educator. Having the opportunity to be a Guiding Teacher to four scholars was an incredible gift and adventure that greatly enhanced the experience of my students and impacted my own teaching style. Each scholar brings a new and unique experience to the classroom, but the joy and rewards are equally great. I learned something very special from each one of them, just as I was trying to teach them a little bit of what I knew. The exchange between the guiding and student teachers can be quite magical at times, and always quite distinctive. An open-minded approach eliminated judgment or punitive action, replaced instead, by a constant and reciprocal flow of ideas, creativity and mutual respect. I gained a tremendous amount of insight about my own practice as a guiding teacher and critically observing each one of the scholars as they developed their style and shaped their practice and approach.

Some basic principles that I followed with all of my scholars were:

> Be open to the experience: Each scholar has something special to offer both you and your students; do not be so rigid and set in your ways that you might stifle his or her growth, creativity or enthusiasm.

> Give support as they need it: Each scholar has specific and unique needs. Some require planning time with you to maintain continuity for your students and get feedback. Others need supplies in order to execute activities, while others need you solely as an enforcer in the classroom. Whatever the needs of the scholar, make sure that your support is specific to the individual and not simply your business as usual. Do not be afraid to step outside of your comfort zone and allow the scholar to really RUN the class.

> Stick to your pedagogy: Remember that you are there to guide those who will hopefully become future educators. Try to share strategies that work for you as a teacher. Discuss your teaching philosophy and how you developed it. Talk to the scholars about why you became a teacher and listen to their views on education. Share your views on education openly, but try to provide a complete and unbiased picture. Be the incredible teacher that you are, and have the courage to share that with them.

These "principles" are pretty basic, but seem to work for every scholar that I have had the opportunity to work with. Iliana Phirippidis and Jena McRae used my lesson and unit plans as a guide to their own planning; they needed a close working relationship that included planning, reflection and critique time, which paid off for us as a team. The students with whom they worked have since graduated, and continue to reflect on that experience with gratitude. Tameka Norris required less planning assistance from me, yet she was fully connected to the students and impacted their high school experience in an extraordinary way by simply sharing so much of herself with all of us. She helped the students find a creative voice with the combination of painting and SAT words. I watched as she pulled from, and nurtured, the students' creativity and expressive voices. Elisabeth Preger used the standards-based vocabulary and brought it to life with her photography background; all she needed from me were a few basic supplies, the occasional enforcement of discipline, and a green light of encouragement. Each scholar offered special and unique qualities to the classroom and made such a tremendous impact on the students at Jordan High School and me. Even after they have left us, their passion, hard work, incredible talent, and energy remained and resonated.

As I look back on that time I have so many beautiful memories, and as I begin to flush them out, there is a commonality: the living energy of creativity and artistic expression. My students read, re-wrote, filmed and produced their own version of Shakespeare's *Macbeth*. The most powerful moment in my Theatre class was a monologue that Cynthia Cruz performed under the direction of Jena McRae. Some very clever and dynamic pieces of art were created using SAT words as the foundation, under the guidance of Tameka Norris; I watched a group of 10th graders develop artistically with photography under Elisabeth Preger's leadership. I felt myself growing and changing as well, and now I can see how much. The Arts educators taught me to stretch myself as a teacher, and they constantly reminded me that our students were capable of accomplishing anything; if I set the goal they would join me at the finish line.

The commitment and energy that the Arts educators brought to the classroom was contagious for my students and me in the classes of 2008 and 2009. Many of the students in the class of 2009 had the opportunity to work with more than one Arts educator and those interactions touched the lives of each student individually. Zindy Valdovinos, Nashalé Andrews, Chané Beard, Shaqueal Adkins, Tysheanna Johnson, Lilliana Serrano, Cynthia Lomeli, Maria Vergara, and Ofelia Padilla have all completed their first year of college at UCLA, CalState Northridge (2), Bethune-Cookman University, San Jose State, CalState San Bernardino (2), UC Davis, and CalState Long Beach respectively. Jenny Vasquez, Yurtiza Sanchez, and Rosa Garcia are attending junior colleges in the Los Angeles area with plans to pursue a four-year degree. Edwin Vizcarra, Grecia Maldonado, Juan Gutierrez, Lourdes Roddriguez, Nubia Virgen, and Julio Ramirez all went directly into the workforce or decided to start their families. I witnessed firsthand the power of Arts in education and the ongoing impact that it has on people's lives. I am in touch with quite a few students who went through the experience. They still talk about how meaningful and memorable it was.

I am no longer in the classroom, but continue my work in the field of education. I am working toward a Doctorate of Philosophy in Education Leadership and Policy Studies at Arizona State University. The experiences that I had as a teacher with my high school students and with ArtsBridge compelled me to extend my reach beyond the walls of a single classroom and into as many as I can touch. In recent conversations with Jordan graduates Shaqueal Adkins, Nashale Andrews and Zindy Valdovinos, they have conveyed how much their experiences in my classroom meant to them and have shaped them. I would love to be able to take all of the credit for that, but I shared my space with some amazing and innovative artists who brought creative energy that was contagious and still lives within us. That gift that lives on from our shared experience with English and the Arts is something that I want more people to have the opportunity to experience.

During this experience, I observed Dr. Amy Shimshon-Santo create and nurture school and community partnerships that were valued by all contributing parties. She provided a strong model for how this work can be done. But it is work. I would like to develop my own method for reaching and working with schools and the community in a long lasting sustainable way, but I am discovering the underlying resistance that exists on both sides of this relationship. The university and the schools are reluctant to take a first leap of faith and join hands, as they have to face the bureaucratic red tape that they each must fight through. Additionally, the individuals who believe in the power of such relationships are often run out of their positions due to a redirection of funds or lack of support. Although there is a sense that Arts and culture matter, there has been no substantial contribution made financially or otherwise to ensure that programs like ArtsBridge continue to thrive and change lives. I know that it is possible and I will work to make it so, once again.

The Arts have a way of changing and shaping you, and everyone deserves the right to have that experience. The essence of the collaborative experience of guiding novice Arts educators can be summed up with this quote from *Wicked*, "Who can say if I've been changed for the better, but because I knew you I have been changed for good."

THE KEY INGREDIENTS
TO A SYMBIOTIC RELATIONSHIP:
TIME, COMMITMENT, AND DEDICATION

Leah Bass-Bayliss

We need the arts to stir creativity and enrich a student's way of knowing, express feelings and ideas that words cannot convey, integrate the fragments of academic life, empower the disabled and give hope to the disenchanted, create community, and build connections across the generations.

- Jane Remer

Reflecting on these words, I am astounded that it is still common for English language learners to be denied the opportunity to participate in quality, standards-based arts instruction due to scheduling issues and "priorities" established by schools. Robert A. Millikan Middle School and Performing Arts Magnet is an award winning school. It is a school that has been designated a California Distinguished School and a California League of Middle Schools School To Watch. Yet Millikan, like so many other secondary schools, is confronted with the lack of quality arts education and ArtsBridge became our ally in resolving the issue. As our school faced mounting budgetary problems, it became apparent that symbiotic partnerships that demanded time, commitment, and dedication, rather than money, and more money, were essential.

As a former central office Arts education administrator, I was painfully aware of the lack of qualified arts educators and the need for aspiring Arts teachers to work beside master Arts teachers. Many meetings and phone conversations with Amy Shimshon-Santo, commiserating about the need for practicum based teacher training and increasing access to the Arts for all students, resulted in a successful three-year partnership.

Our first year together was certainly the most challenging. Developing a structure for aspiring educators to visit classrooms in which Arts were being taught and receive feedback was a major issue. How do we find time for master teachers to meet, collaborate, and discuss with no budget? We scheduled time during our school buy back days for Amy to share her vision with the Millikan staff and then provided her with general information about the school and building in time for me to conduct an orientation for Millikan prior to classroom visitations. Amy and I realized quickly that her novice arts teachers, who were university students, needed to create lesson plans and share them with my Millikan teachers for feedback prior to implementing them with youth. Finally, we added time throughout the observation and teaching day for students to speak with their mentors and ask questions about observations. Teachers were willing to give their conference periods and lunchtime to make this invaluable exchange occur.

Getting the lesson plans in a timely manner, getting teacher comments, and then distributing this information to all parties involved proved to be especially challenging. There just weren't enough hours in the day for people not to feel pressured by the deadlines; and some teachers, though well meaning, discouraged and frustrated the aspiring educators. Amy and I quickly realized that this would be an area of revision.

Scheduling orientation, observations, and teaching time proved to be monumental! As an administrator I must prioritize time, and there is never enough time at a school site for all that must be done. Amy was faced with trying to fit the many different schedules of her students into both our school schedule and the general school schedule at UCLA. We realized that all parties involved had to be flexible and reachable via phone, email, and/or text message. Amy and I decided that we had to make it work - and so we did.

After completing the initial observations and trial lessons, we decided upon two long-term residencies for our English-language learner students and our DRW (Developing Readers and Writers) programs. Students in these programs were denied access to electives due to scheduling and a "double block" of English instruction. The aspiring Arts educators from UCLA would be faced with working with the teachers to develop an instructional unit that incorporated the standards of the selected Arts discipline with the instructional modules from High Point (English language learner curriculum) or DRW (literacy based curriculum for students experiencing extreme difficulty with English language arts). The mentor teacher would be faced with learning about the arts discipline, while the arts educator would be faced with learning the basics of pedagogy coupled with a basic understanding of literacy skills that make up a large part of the High Point and DRW curriculum.

Laurel Bybee, in her essay, "Discovering Language Assets Through Design," refers to Beverly Tatum's ABC approach to teaching. As I read her essay I found myself focusing on the "B" – Building a Community. It is this arena in which each Arts educator excelled and that these students needed the most.

To understand this comment, one must be given a clear picture of the Millikan student population. Millikan is a school of 2,000 students, 1,000 of whom are a part of the performing arts academy and/or the performing arts magnet who participate in an arts elective. Of the remaining 1,000 approximately 500 of them are in one of the traditional academies which include: civics, science, visual communications and math. The remaining 500 included the 300 English language learners, the 60 DRW students, and others who chose not be a part of any of the other groups on campus. The only students on campus without an elective are the English language learners and DRW students. These students represented the only group of students with no opportunity to participate in the Arts, and, therefore, no opportunity to perform in any school-wide or small learning community presentation.

I was very impressed with the artist educators and their willingness to take on this challenge and in a few short weeks one could feel the sense of community growing. A visit to the classroom found the students engaged, focused, and excited about what they were doing. Sometimes I would visit the classrooms and walk around asking the students to tell me what they were working on. Sometimes I'd stop the teachers in the cafeteria who would immediately begin telling me stories about various class happenings. Sometimes they'd complain about the artist arriving late or not coming. Sometimes they would excitedly talk about something that was produced by one of the students. Sometimes they would have an "aha" moment to share. Regardless of the question or inquiry, everyone - students and teachers - had something to say. Everybody cared about what was happening!

For each group of students, the program peaked at a different place. For the students learning salsa, the high point was the performance and winning trophies in the school-wide Ballroom Blast competition. For the groups working with visual arts, it was the symposium and knowing that their work would be shared at UCLA. The entire class seemed excited that their classmates would be representing the school at a special event. Both teachers were as excited as their students, and both also presented at a statewide middle school conference. By the end of the year, both were asking what would be coming next year. We engaged in many reflective conversations about the value of the arts and the changes they saw in their students.

Data, data, and more data in the form of test scores seem to be the lone measuring rod for student achievement. I certainly value the information provided by standardized tests but I think it's a mistake to ignore smiles and laughter where there were little or none. I think it's a mistake to ignore the change in attitude and the level of engagement for students who previously expressed nothing but dislike for school. As I watched one teacher rehearsing her students for the performance and the other teacher working with several students for the symposium, I was amazed at the change in their demeanor.

Since that first year, we have added an evaluative tool for the mentor teachers to complete, and most lessons were filmed for the artist educators to review. As I reflect on that first year, I think about the lessons that we have learned. It is important that both organizations identify their capabilities, specific needs, goals, and objectives. Communication is a must and requires establishment of norms for sharing information. I wish that we could continue to revise, improve, and touch more students.

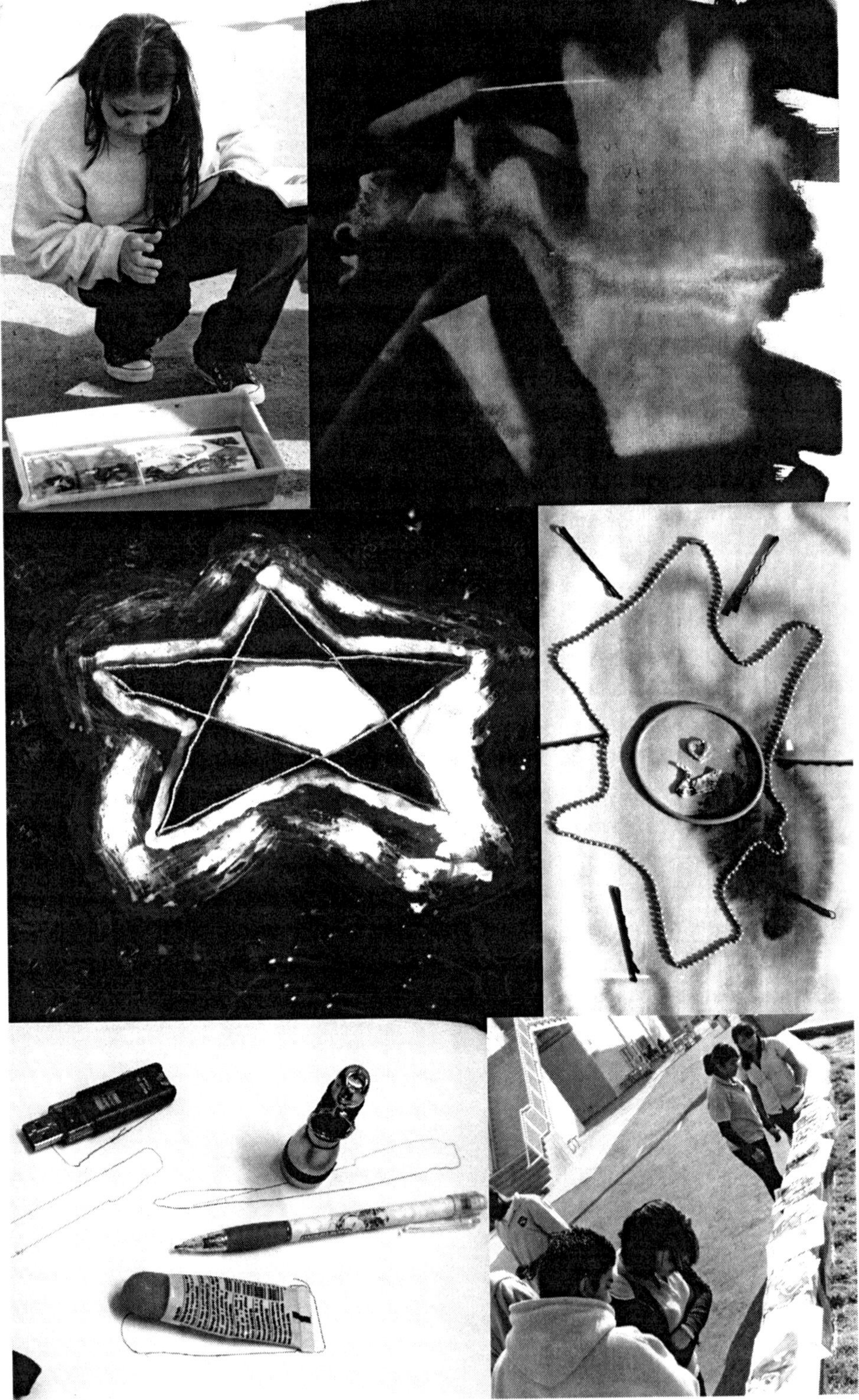

PROCESS REFLECTIONS

Process Section Overview

Arts educators don't enter the classroom empty handed. Long before they meet their prospective students, they have defined intentions for teaching and learning, articulated key questions, planned and sequenced lessons and units, developed assessments to evaluate student learning, and learned as much as possible about the school and community. However, the shift from preparing to teach to actually entering a classroom with real students is transformative for new educators. For the first time in their lives, they may be addressed by their last name first, and the change in roles liberates something deep inside them. What do they know? What can they share? All the preparation in the world is only that--preparation. During this exciting time in the life of new teachers, they are forced to put thought into action, to transform an individual plan into a valuable group experience. It takes a great facilitator to transform a big idea, and sequence of lessons, into a transformative experience. One must be clear. One must be engaging. One must be patient. This is when reflective teaching, participating in a professional learning community, and receiving guidance from experienced Arts educators and community members can support the aspirations of emerging educators.

In "Critical Pedagogy Through Cultural Pedagogy," Mehvish Arifeen discusses how she imbued music education with historical, cultural, and social meaning by teaching Pakistani choral music to young singers at Washington Preparatory High School in South Los Angeles. Marina Magalhães describes her "Breakthrough" while teaching Pan-Latino dance at Lynwood High School. After initial difficulties, Magalhães finally began to trust in her own creative style, put her theory of social change into practice, and foster an enjoyable and empowering learning experience for her students. In her attempt to teach color theory to elementary school students at Jefferson Elementary School, Amy Chen realized that her students had not been exposed to the color schemes of climates outside of their local setting. Her essay, "Warm Climate/Cool Climate: Teaching Color Theory to Elementary Students," describes how her classroom became a place for children to travel beyond the boundaries of their neighborhood through the imagination. Her teaching partner, Shannon Hickey, writes about the importance of having a professional learning community of teachers in "Two Heads Are Better Than One." She argues that new teachers can fight the feeling of classroom isolation through community support. Ellen Mulvanny's article recounts how teaching youth at West Adams Preparatory High School helped her realize the key significance of decision making in architectural design.

These essays highlight the revelations and challenges of cultivating a community partnership and capture the raw awakening of new arts educators as they are launched into the classroom. The thoughtful teaching epiphanies shared by the authors expose the confrontation between theory and practice, while facilitating student learning in dance, music, art, and architecture.

CREATIVE PEDAGOGY
THROUGH CRITICAL PEDAGOGY

Mehvish Arifeen

I know I can be what I wanna be
If I work hard at it I'll be where I wanna be.

- NaS

Arts education is defined by the relationship between the imagination, achievement and pedagogy. This relationship is not limited to teaching art for the sake of art, and is, in fact, a pedagogical technique that integrates arts with education so that students develop a sound understanding of the historical, cultural, and social complexities that surround them. Cynthia Weiss states, "We want to help children by giving them every possible tool for making meaning out of a complex world" (Weiss 2008:3). Integrating education and the Arts allows students to express their emotions and critical thoughts with comfort using music, dance, poetry, art, or spoken word, and to articulate their sentiments by connecting the Art with their realities.

Unfortunately, not all institutions can afford the resources that help create an effective arts education program and, therefore, keep the academics and the Arts segregated from each other. Many people find it hard to fully comprehend how instrumental Arts integration can be in student learning and in understanding student achievement. The irony, however, exists in the fact that schools in low-income neighborhoods are the ones that need arts integrated with education the most. The main reason is that students who attend inner city schools are struggling against real obstacles to their safety and success that comes with social marginalization. The majority of the students enrolled in schools in South and East Los Angeles are Latinos and African Americans. Students who encounter tough economic and social realities everyday deserve an education where information is being given to them with a purpose and is relevant to their understanding of the world and their struggles. Students deserve a platform through which they can express themselves comfortably and openly through academia in a school environment. In this way, instead of viewing the school as an institution that is alienated from reality and their personal struggles, the student will feel that they are able to express themselves in a positive way through school.

As an Arts educator, I have found that the most challenging issue I have had to deal with is, how does one educate better through the Arts? What is it about the Arts, that, when integrated with education, gives learning, imagination and knowledge a whole new meaning? In my teaching experience I have come to realize the answer to this very significant question. It appears to me that the reason why Arts education is so instrumental in helping students realize themselves and their role in their surroundings is because it is a means of expression shaped by history and the cultural and social events that define human beings in their respective environments. Duncan - Andrade and Morrell would define this method as critical pedagogy:

> *Critical pedagogues, drawing on social and critical educational theory and cultural studies, examine schools in their historical context and as part of the existing social and political fabric that characterizes the dominant society. They challenge the assumption that schools function as major sites of social and economic mobility. Instead, they suggest that schooling must be analyzed as a cultural and historical process in which students are positioned within asymmetrical relations of power on the basis of specific race, class and gender groupings (Duncan-Andrade and Morrell 2008:23).*

I tried to approach my teaching assignment at Washington Preparatory High School from the perspective of a critical pedagogue. My goal has been to share an art form that the students feel they can relate to, and express themselves through, while being exposed to a new language, cultural history and art form. The main theme of my classes has been Punjabi Sufi poetry through song. The poetry mainly addresses social issues and phenomena such as a woman's right to marriage or to love. Through music, the students also learned about the atrocities and hardships faced by a lot of women in places such as Pakistan. In my classes so far, I have tried to draw parallels between the issues of choice and privilege faced by individuals in my culture and the students in my class. It was interesting to see that most of the students in the choir feel that even though they have their own struggles, they are still privileged to be where they are as young women. For me, this is a positive reflection of the lessons that I am teaching to my students. It is my goal to help them feel empowered, strong, confident and motivated, so that they dream big and set meaningful goals for themselves, so that they too can further pass on cultural enrichment through their own art forms. Also the teaching process has helped me develop creative pedagogy through critical pedagogy, where I am able to teach my art form in creative ways of using methods and techniques, such as call and response, which is not indigenous to this musical tradition.

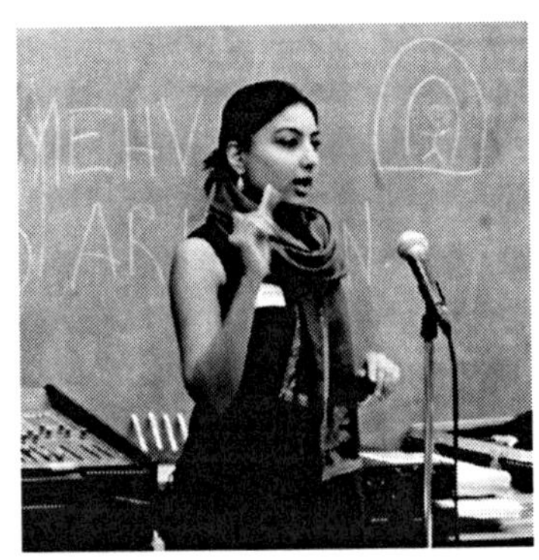

"DO WHAT YOU WANT –
JUST KNOW WHY YOU'RE DOING IT!"
ARCHITECTURAL EDUCATION AS
SPATIAL REASONING FOR TEENS

Ellen Mulvanny

I came to the ArtsBridge Program at UCLA during the second year of pursuing my Masters of Architecture degree. After six months in the program including critical reading, instructional modeling, sequential lesson planning, school observations, and teaching sample workshops, I offer the following essay as a reflection on my own work-in-progress.

My first round of "desk crits" with the students at West Adams Preparatory High School came two weeks into my residency. "Desk crits" are individual student-teacher meetings about the student's work-in-progress. As I went from student to student, I tried to tailor questions and feedback to the tasks they laid out for themselves in designing their schools: "Your school is near a lake so I like that you've designed so much of it outdoors." "If that's the performance area for your music school do you want the classrooms close by to share in the music or further away to buffer noise transfer?" "Why does a school for zombies require circular classrooms?" Finally a student asked me: "Do we have to have a reason for everything we do?"

I think this question comes up for every architecture student at some point and in some form. As first-year graduate students in architecture come around in the discipline, you hear the typical epiphanies: "You can do anything you want as long as you have a reason ... Go ahead and do it, just be prepared to explain why…" My advice to my high school students followed the same creed: "Maybe you don't want five classrooms in your school, despite the program requirements; maybe you want to argue that your school only needs three because the playing fields outside serve the same function as classrooms…*Do what you want, just know why you're doing it.*"

If we're all just doing what we want, Why do we need graduate schools, college programs, and 12-week high school level architecture workshops anyway? If any idea can be a good idea, what is an education in architectural design *really?*

Simply put, a design education is about communicating those good ideas. It is about communicating ideas through drawings, photographs, collage and any number of traditional and non-traditional media. This is especially true for architecture – where we don't build the product of the design ourselves, but rather we create an idea of a building or space and communicate it through plans, sections, perspective renderings and models. So do architecture students have to have a reason for everything we do? Yes. And we have to have reasons for everything we don't do.

This can be overwhelming for any student (at any level) used to the sequential processes of the scientific method or drill-based learning, which teach you to follow a clear linear process to a successful end. A design education teaches a different way of thinking – a different language for problem solving in which you create the problem before you create the solution – and the two remain in a constant dialectic. Guided, reasoned and intentional decision-making is the best tool we have for: a) navigating this process without losing our minds, and b) communicating this process without our audience losing theirs. Just as a change in design reverberates in all its representational manifestations, it can dramatically alter the architectural problem at hand as well. Intentionality in this case works in both directions. So, if you're designing a school for zombies and you want circular classrooms, you need to be able to explain why – and maybe it means changing the nature of said zombies. (They compulsively run in circles as it turns out.)

If architectural design is about a clear communication of ideas - to the extent that problem and solution become parallel, subservient processes – then teaching architectural design is about teaching students to render, process, and present these ideas. So the question becomes: "How do you teach students to be creative, while, at the same time teaching them to clearly delineate their ideas about space in a rational, communicable manner?" Or, "How do you teach students to have a reason for everything they want to do?"

The issue is one of translation. Students need to understand their ideas about space in communicable terms in order to design space in an effective manner (again, we see the bi-directional nature of the process). In most design media, students learn a method of making as part of the design process – there is a set of learned steps and techniques for painting, drawing, sculpting. The creativity then, lies mostly in the content of the work. In architecture too, there are established methods of representation, but none wholly constitutes "the design" in the way a photograph or painting does. So when you paint a painting, you communicate the content of the painting. But when you design a space, you must draw, diagram and build that space in a way that translates the underlying content across these media.

This special emphasis on the communication of the design is what drives the hyper-awareness of the architectural design process – it is why you have to have a reason for every decision you make. My high school students at West Adams not only intuited this process of questioning the architectural problem while searching for the solution, but they taught me to better understand (and therefore communicate) the steps I take towards my own degree in architecture. Their questions demanded a clear communication of the abstractions I take for granted daily. By asking "why?" my students taught me all the reasons I'm doing what I want.

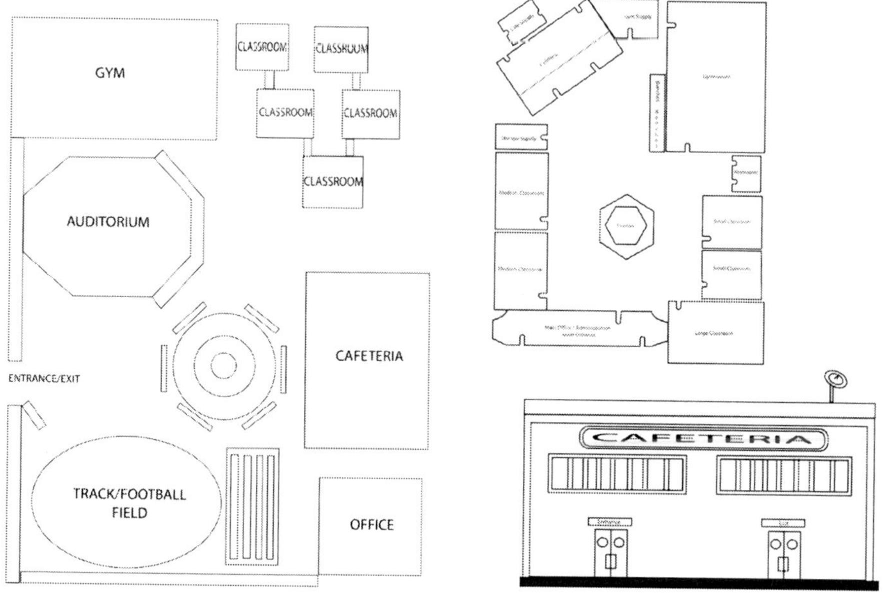

GYM
CLASSROOM
CLASSROOM
CLASSROOM
CLASSROOM
CLASSROOM
AUDITORIUM
ENTRANCE/EXIT
CAFETERIA
TRACK/FOOTBALL FIELD
OFFICE
CAFETERIA

WARM CLIMATE / COOL CLIMATE: TEACHING COLOR THEORY TO ELEMENTARY SCHOOL STUDENTS IN COMPTON

Amy Chen

I first heard of the ArtsBridge program in the summer before my third year at UCLA. As an art major, I was excited at the opportunity to share knowledge and passion to with youth with little or no exposure to Art. Within the first few lessons teaching at Jefferson Elementary, a whole new world opened up. Upon meeting the students, and talking with them, the abstract idea of "exposure" suddenly had faces, names, and a history. What each of my students shared was a passion to learn.

When I first arrived at Jefferson Elementary School in Compton to observe the classrooms and teachers with my teaching partner Shannon, we saw that each classroom was a portable, their playground was the concrete that connected the classrooms, and there seemed to be only one handball court around.

The following week when we began teaching and got situated with our second graders, we realized that had no understanding of color theory. During one lesson, Shannon printed out examples of cold and warm environments to portray the colors that represented their temperatures. We had a picture of a mountain, a desert, an ocean, and a beach. When we showed the pictures in class, with a projector that didn't even portray all the vibrant colors, all the kids' eyes opened wide and they yelled out in excitement. I couldn't understand it. My initial thought was just of bewilderment. It wasn't as if the images were of specific famous places – they were roughly generic. What was so special? Their excitement made me realize that this could have been their first time witnessing anything close to what a beach or desert was and that their neighborhoods might have been the only places they had ever seen. The power of exposing these second grade students to new places was invigorating, and in the next activity we saw an immediate impact in their illustrations of hot and cold environments.

Shannon and I talked about this later and concluded that in the next lesson we would continue teaching color, but show not only pictures of environments, but of cultural places, such as the Great Wall of China, the Taj Mahal, the pyramids of Egypt, and so forth. Once again, the class went wild, constantly talking about where in the world these monuments were. They were even surprised to find out that the Tulum Ruins were located in Mexico. I never imagined such an impact until I saw these same monuments, shown briefly in our presentation, later resurfacing within the student's drawings. There were pyramids bathed in reds, oranges and yellows, structures that resembled the Taj Mahal and the Tulum Ruins, in purples, greens, and blues. The images had stuck in their heads and were already being creatively churned inside their minds and out through their hands. They were already learning how to draw something new based on sight. If something visual could stimulate the way our students draw, what else could stimulate them? What about other senses? For example, how might texture or audio influence their drawings? What else could we expose them to? These new experiences of cultural exposure can lead to an infinite number of further possibilities.

It was exposure to these second graders that refueled my own desire to teach and to expose, to bring forth anything I can to inspire them, even one picture at a time. Pictures of different cultures and places are a good way to expose students to the diversity in our world. In the future, I will continue to expose my students to the outside world through art and teach them to value their own personal creative process.

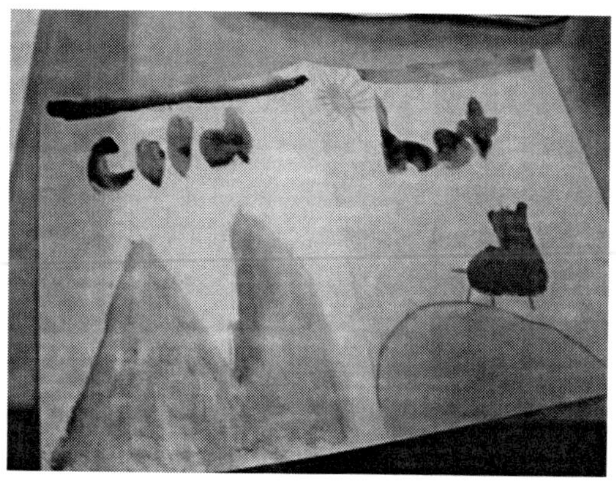

TWO HEADS ARE BETTER THAN ONE

Shannon Hickey

After a long hot drive across Los Angeles freeways, Amy Chen and I finally made it to Jefferson Elementary in Compton, California. I popped my trunk, and we unloaded our loot of yellow, red, and blue tempera paint, white construction paper, and colored makers. We were armed with a carefully thought out lesson plan, PowerPoint presentation, and closed toed shoes. Amy and I were seemingly ready to step into our second grade classes and start to teach our students about color mixing. Truthfully, no matter how prepared we are for each lesson and activity, things never go as expected or predicted, and that has been the beauty of my teaching experience thus far.

When I originally set out to teach Ms. Sneath's second grade class, I thought I would only be teaching drawing, line, shapes, and figure making. However this is not all that my residency has turned out to be. One, I am not teaching alone, and this has been a blessing. My teaching partner, Amy, is amazing. The bigger issue in having a teaching partner is the support system. I never realized before I started my residency, how many uncertainties and insecurities would come with the job. When you go into a classroom you are standing in front of students looking to you for direction. This alone can be intimidating. Secondly, when you have a carefully planed out lesson, as you teach it, you are trying to communicate meaning to your students. But when that meaning does not translate to your students, you can feel lost. In a few of our lessons I have ended knowing my students did not understand the concept. Where do you go from there? It is during these situations that having a teaching partner, or a community of teachers, can be the best thing in the world.

Amy and I have the common goal to teach our second grade classes the art of color mixing. By creating our lesson plans together, we make more cohesive and efficient lessons. When things go wrong, or a method of teaching does not get through to our students, we are able to problem solve together. Imagine if every teacher had the benefit of working with a partner, or in groups, to share their experiences and concerns? I believe that if teachers were to communicate with fellow teachers in their schools, or perhaps in neighboring schools, they would make each other aware of effective and ineffective teaching methods and practices. Not to mention the emotional support that a collaboration of teachers could give one another.

In my own future teaching practice I hope to use collaboration with other teachers in order to better myself and give my students all the tools they can gather from their own learning experience. As, for my experience in the ArtsBridge program, having my teaching partner by my side has made all the difference. Through ArtsBridge we now have an unspoken bond where we always have each other's back, no matter the situation. In the end, having a teaching partner is a plus; however having a newly developed friendship is even better!

I have grown so much as a person from the ArtsBridge experience, and I am only half way through. On a teaching level, I have realized that my students are brilliant in their own right. However, what I have been exposed to in my life and what they have been exposed to are two completely different things. So, when I bring my experiences into teaching I cannot assume that my students will understand what I am teaching them. I have learned that I need to plan and sequence instruction even more than I had previously thought. Also, trying different methods of teaching the same subject or concept is the best way to reach all of your students. These teaching points are relevant to my personal teaching practice; however the more important realization from my teaching experience is that there is no need to teach alone - or feel alone as a teacher. On the contrary, a community of educators can give teachers a wonderful tool to help create beneficial lessons for their students.

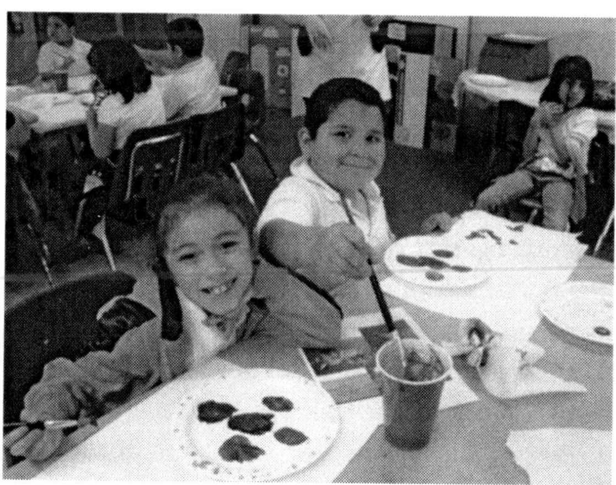

MY BREAKTHROUGH

Marina Magalhães

I came to the ArtsBridge program in my third undergraduate year as a World Arts and Cultures Major with a Dance Concentration and Women's Studios Minor. During my third week teaching the salsa technique of Casino Rueda to a mixed-grade dance class at Lynwood High School, I had a breakthrough about what it means to practice what I preach, to put into action progressive rhetoric and ideas. My students taught me about the inaccessibility of my own progressive ideals and how the joy and challenge of dance can serve as an empowering entry point to progressive academia. This essay is a reflection on my teaching experience so far.

I had that breakthrough somewhere between saying "good morning" and "goodbye" to my students on the day of March 12th, 2009. Between the hours of 8:10 and 9:50 a.m., I learned what it was to be a good teacher, and I learned exactly what I was preaching to my students - that highly sensitive improvisation, really listening to your instincts, and having acute awareness of your environment and the people in it made for the strongest performers. That day, I performed as the best teacher I could be.

Up until that lesson, I was struggling with being comfortable and confident in my role as a dance educator, a teacher, an authority figure, a so-called expert in my field. I had to learn to trust myself and my experience. I realized that my own creativity, set of experiences, knowledge, and artistic interest are what makes me a good teacher. That is what I have to bring to the table, and those are things of value that I can offer my students.

I also realized that I had been getting caught up in the jargon and rhetoric of the progressive ideas I was trying to cover in class, including ideas of hybridity, commodification, resistance, and oppression. I was trying to get my students to engage with these ideas on the level that I am used to engaging with them, at a very conceptual, intellectual, and theoretical level. By doing so I was having a hard time getting their attention, getting them interested in the material, having them enjoy the technique and the dancing, and gaining their trust and respect.

It became clear to me that there is gap in the progressive movement that I am so passionate about and involved in. It can be inaccessible to the people and communities that it claims to be representing and speaking for.

How do I transmit ideas of resistance, pushing back, having your voice heard, democracy, cultural commodification, dynamics of power, and social oppression to teenagers, teenagers who are obviously a part of all these things, but who perhaps do not realize it or have the words to articulate their placement and situation, teenagers who are more concerned with looking stupid, weird, or different in front of their classmates when learning new dances, cultures, music?

Recently, I went back to the basics: having fun with the dance, smiling to each and every student as they walked in, asking them how they felt about what we've been doing, and being quiet when I wanted to get their attention. I replaced that with being stern with them and scorning them for laughing and talking while I tried to tell them about all the beautiful complexities and contradictions of dance and dance theory.

I finally realized that less is more.

It became clear to me that the reason why I had been feeling so ineffective as a teacher had nothing to do with my students, but with the kind of energy and attitude that I was bringing into the classroom. I was walking into the classroom distrusting my lesson plan and asking myself, "How am I going to transmit all of these really complex concepts to them? Are they going to get it? Is it going to be relevant? What if I don't know enough to teach them?" Their behavior and comments, telling me that they were too tired, didn't want to dance, didn't get it, and didn't want to try, were only in response to my lack of energy. As soon as I changed that, they were completely willing to engage, participate, try hard, have fun, and take something away from the class.

I started to compromise. I would find things that they were familiar with, good at, and used these as an entry point to talk about new ideas, including the complicated concepts I wanted to introduce to them and cover in class. For example, during the warm-up, instead of using all salsa music, I put in some of what I like (Brazilian contemporary music), some of what they like (John Legend, Lauryn Hill, Juanes) and made it relevant by doing our usual movements and techniques to those songs. Now they had an aesthetic entry point into the material.

I also realized that even though their technical dance level was introductory, this group of students had experience in choreography and making dances. So, in addition to drilling them on the Casino Rueda technique, I decided to trust their abilities enough to teach them more advanced steps, including how to switch partners. They learned this in ten minutes, once I broke it down enough and was patient and trusting.

Since Casino Rueda is based on a Call and Response format, where the leader calls out the steps and the group responds by doing them, I had the students come up with their own dance calls, which would be named after them. Each person had to call their step, and the rest of the group had to respond by doing and saying it back to them.

After doing this, I asked them how they felt about Casino Rueda and if their feelings towards it had changed or improved at all. They said they loved it and had so much fun, because they were able to express themselves while creating their own Rueda calls. I used their comments as a way to connect back to one of the Visual and Performing Arts Standards (VAPA) in a historical and cultural context. I shared with them, "Well, that's exactly how Rueda originated in Cuba. A group of kids from the neighborhood got together and decided they were going to come up with all these different calls. That's exactly what we all just did in this room. Reenact that."

After saying this, I heard ohs and ahs from around the room, saw smiles on people's faces, and joined in their applause as the students walked out of the classroom chattering and laughing with each other. Together we engaged in the physical translation of resistance by learning to trust, lead and follow our Casino Rueda partners; we redefined cultural commodification by reclaiming Casino Rueda and creating dances based on our own Rueda calls; and we practiced cultural hybridity by making the Casino Rueda calls bilingual and making our own Rueda calls reflective of our hybrid backgrounds. Through all of this, we rejected the institutional oppression of uncreative school curricula by empowering ourselves through our own dance making and community building.

I am finally beginning to understand what the title of our program, ArtsBridge, is referring to: the bridge between cultural theory and dance practice, what we talk about outside the classroom and what we do inside it. Somewhere between walking in and out of that classroom, my students enabled the breakthrough about my own craft, ideals, and values. I now feel more able to both walk the walk and talk the talk.

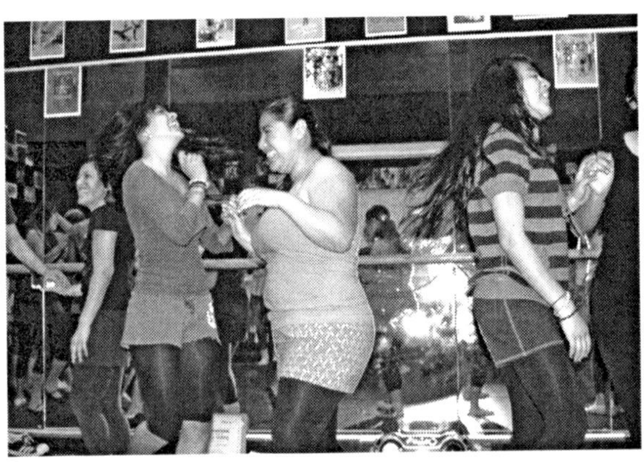

MY BREAKTHROUGH

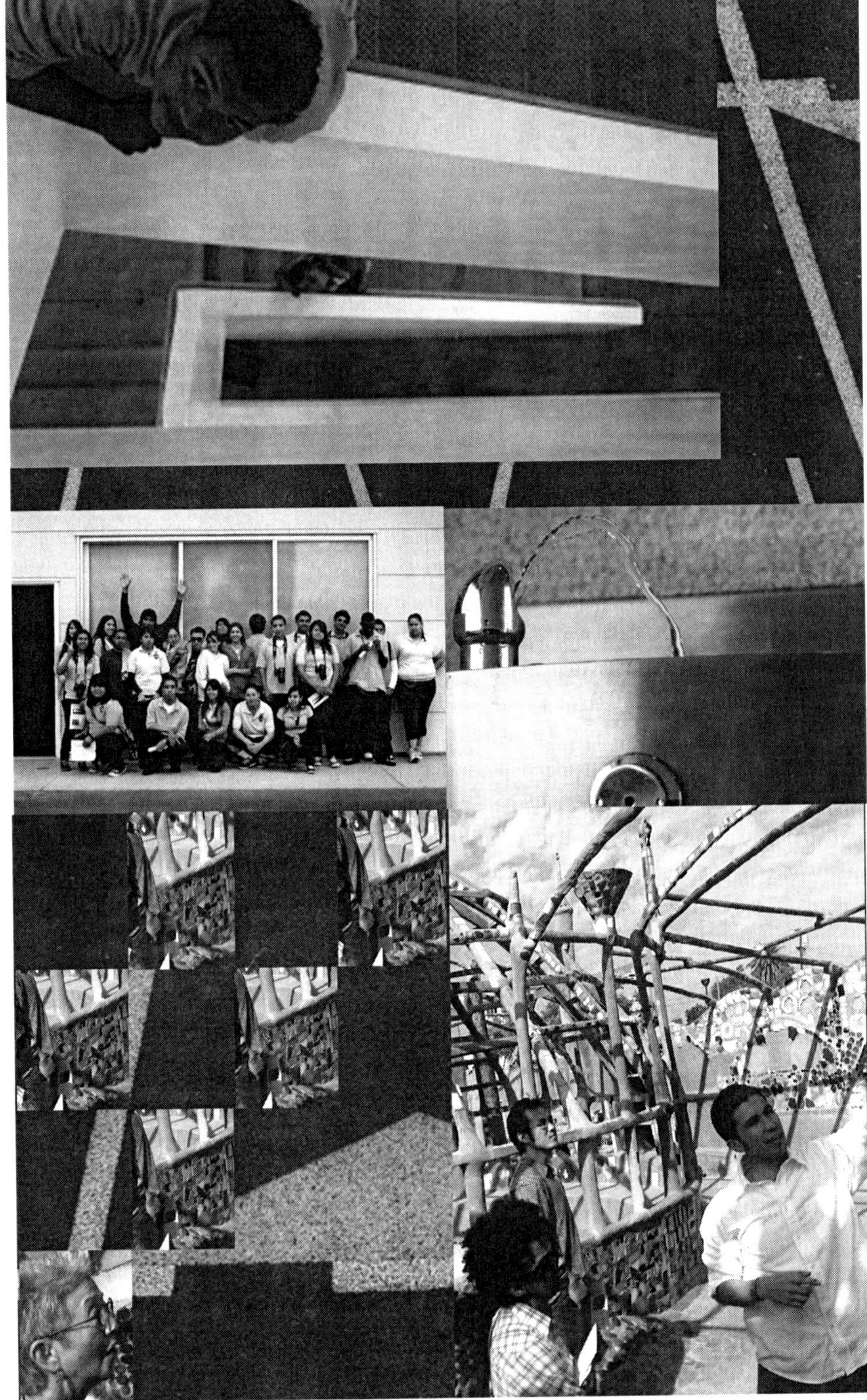

CROSSING LEARNING CONTEXTS

Translate Section Overview

Having designed a stunning aerial view map of Los Angeles depicting his path from UCLA (where he studied Design | Media Arts) to South L.A. (where he taught applied arts to students at John Muir Middle School), Leon Hong looked perplexed. "How can I better describe the differences between here and there?" he asked me. At that moment, in marched Guiding Teacher Lorien Eck and three students from Eck's class Leon was teaching with Muskan Srivastava. They were meeting in my office to rehearse for their collaborative presentation at our annual symposium. "Let's ask them!" I suggested. The young women, who had never previously visited UCLA, easily explained the distinctions. Gabriela stated that their school was smaller, and their neighborhood (near Slauson and Vermont Avenues) was filled with different immigrant groups. UCLA, they had ascertained, was bigger, cleaner, had more trees, and people looked lonelier too. For me, that moment confirmed young people's awareness and ease giving voice to the inequalities that often make adults cringe or hide. Any community partnership that unites different learning communities inevitably requires translating across contexts. The borders we cross may be linguistic, geographic, cultural, economic, or political. Border crossing requires that participants confront themselves and their differences in a new way. The essays in this section grapple with how people perceive, translate, and negotiate across the different learning contexts at home, school, and the university.

In addition to analytical pieces, this section includes student reflections and photos about where they go to school. Iris Schneider, photographer and former photo editor for the *Los Angeles Times*, met with me to map out how we could include photo journalism in our community building efforts. This desire was inspired in part by an unfortunate event involving a fight between youth from two of our partner schools during an unrelated field trip to a museum in greater Los Angeles. The guiding teachers and I saw the need to create a space that would allowed youth to move beyond local boundaries that are delineated and enforced by gang associations. The informal map of gang territories limit the mobility of youth in Los Angeles and their access to public programs. Oftentimes residents cannot take advantage of local resources if they require crossing borders through neighborhoods where they might be in danger of unwarranted retaliation. Our intervention to this problem was to work across neighborhoods through photography. We created a visual storytelling project focusing on "School As I See It" that was held after-school at David Starr Jordan High School thanks to the kindness of Martin Cheeseborough (Director of the Media Art Center), Iris Schneider, and Canon Cameras. Youth, parents, and teachers from David Starr Jordan High School, West Adams Preparatory High School, Lynwood High School, and Bunche Middle School worked together in consort with UCLA students. Over the year, we used the camera to let students and parents depict insiders' perspectives of school and community. Excerpts from a series of still photography videos produced by the group (e.g., *The Feeling of Opportunity, Road to Success, When There's a Will There's A Way, It Is Never Too Late to Learn*, and *Making a Better Future)* are included in this section and available as short movies on YouTube.

Immigration status is an issue that emerged for many of the students participating in the program, and for many university students as well. Our partnerships offered sequential instruction in the arts, as well as field trips and academic shadowing opportunities.[1] One day I was invited to watch a student theater production at George Washington Carver Middle School facilitated by the Center Theater Group. Students titled their play "Welcome to the Border, Now Go Home." I invited the young thespians to campus to present their play and speak directly with undocumented university students to publicize and address educational rights for undocumented students. This problematic is discussed in greater detail in the essay, "Dramatizing Borders."

Cynthia Wennstrom's work, "The Language of Creativity," analyzes her visual arts residency with Directed Reading and Writing (DRW) students at Millikan Middle School. Wennstrom was first paired with classroom teacher Betty Poncin for a sample class where Wennstrom led a lesson in composition and line. Drawing from Kandinsky's inspiration in music, she guided the students through a collage activity focusing on the eye, line, and emotion. It was observing class that day that I first met Jasmine Hardaway who composed a collage resembling a bird in flight and sang a freedom song to the group inspired by music from her church. She had organically made the connection between line and emotion, visual art and music. After Hardaway's discovery, Wennstrom and Poncin decided to work together to use visual arts instruction to support literacy for young people who were denied an arts elective due to a requirement that DRW students receive a double block of English instruction. This same mandate also applies to students in English Language Learning (ELL) classrooms. After six months of study, Wennstrom's students' language comprehension test scores improved from 2-5 grade levels – a great success given the students' struggles with reaching grade level reading and writing benchmarks. Concerned about tampering, the Los Angeles Unified School District required that the class retest in English, and the students exceeded expectations a second time. Poncin described the event as resembling a *Stand a Deliver* success story for her language arts students. Principal Bass-Bayliss made sure that the teachers spread the word by presenting student learning outcomes at the California League of Middle Schools Conference in Sacramento the following year.

Both Alicia Paniagua's interview, "If My Voice Could Fly," which discusses her experience teaching salsa dance to middle school students, and Laurel Bybee's essay, "Discovering Language Assets Through Design," demonstrate how useful the Arts can be to sparking language acquisition for students in ELL classrooms. In "Media Literacy in Middle School," history teacher Lisa Nuñez observed her students grapple with expressing themselves visually in a design | media arts class, and found visual expression useful to the way they understood and represented historical knowledge.

Given the utility of the arts in invigorating learning, the work in this section calls into question a common practice of denying arts education to students who may need it the most. The places where we live and study, and the languages we speak or silence in schools, reflect decisions about what knowledge counts, what knowledge does not, and how people learn. The writing in this section suggests a central role for the imagination in learning in school and in the community.

Notes

1   *Academic shadowing offers children and youth a chance to shadow, or spend time with, a university student on campus and experience college life.*

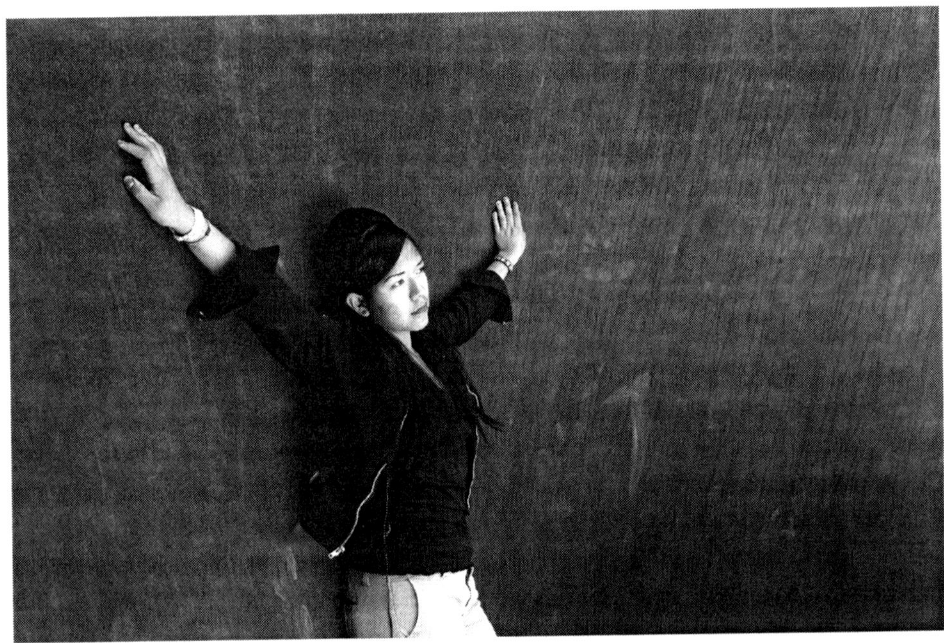

Let me tell you a little bit about West Adams High School: the programs, the clubs, the school structure, the staff, the freedom to do what any other student would have loved to do, from video production to design. That is what all students should have as an option, but don't. Unfortunately, in my neighborhood, we never had that option. The connections I have now in this school...Well, it's amazing. And until the day I say I graduated and headed to UCLA, it will set my imagination and my dreams to dust. Now I'm into what I want to do - the arts. I sense the feeling of opportunity and the thought of doing something with my life that I never had before.

- PAMELA VELASQUEZ

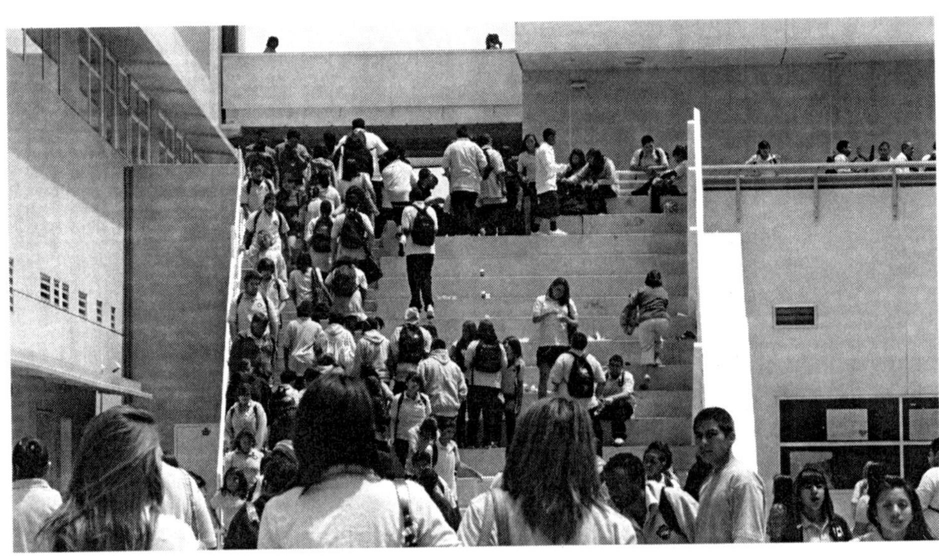

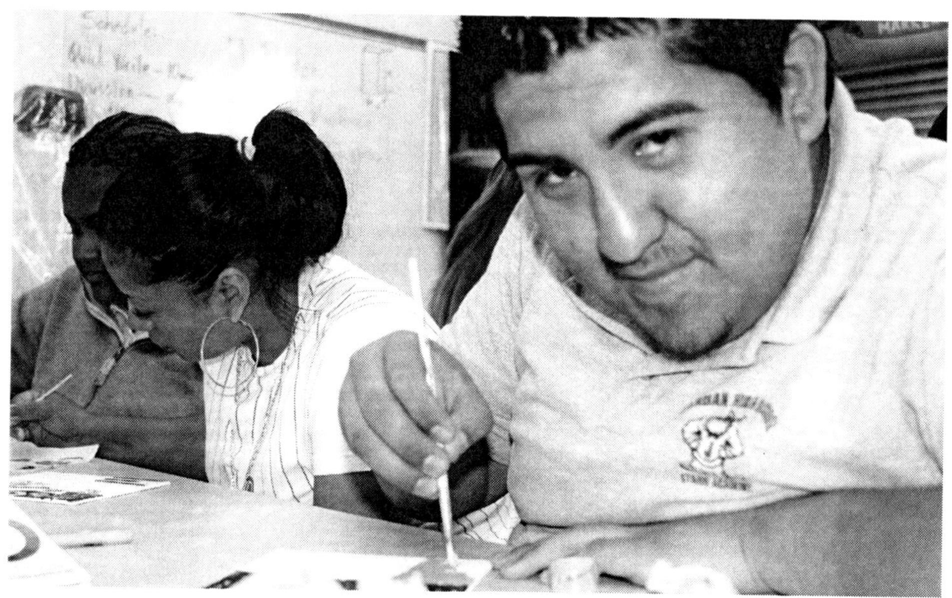

Life at Jordan High School is not all fun and games. For many people there is a yellow brick road that takes them in the right path. For us, we must all work together to build that yellow brick road, not only for us, but also for those who are to come after. We can only build this road with hard work and devotion to ourselves and to our community to reach our goals of success. Fairy godmothers and fairy godfathers in the form of teachers, help us along the way. Everyday they give us the tools we need to grow, and together we can hopefully one day complete the road to success.

- EDWIN VIZCARRA

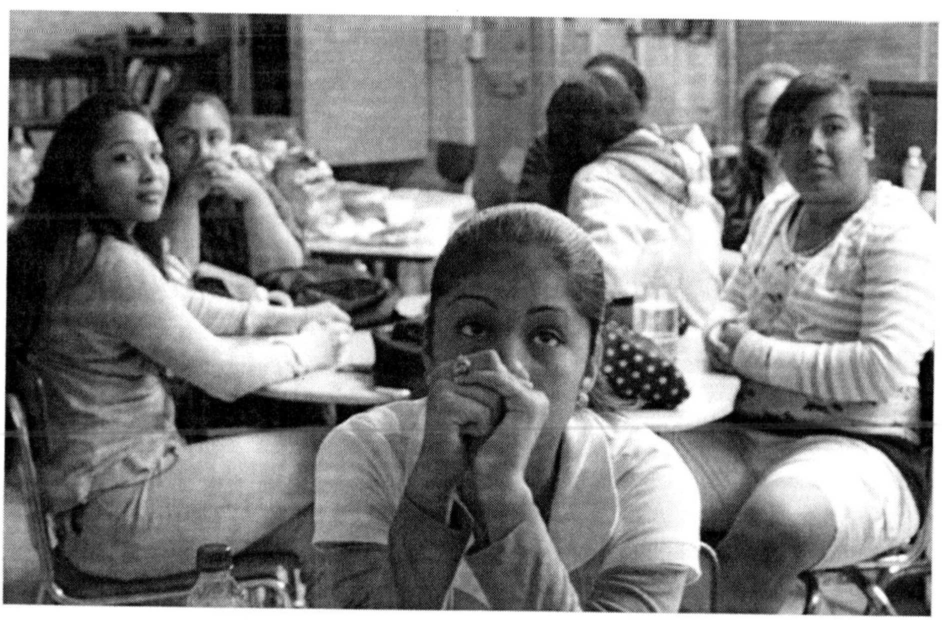

I always heard that "where there is a will there is a way." But to me, it was meant for other people but not for me. My life revolved around my husband, my children, and a home. I lamented not having studied when I was young and single. But one day the opportunity knocked at my door because of the new administration at my son's school, and it changed my life making me relook at the phrase "where there is a will there is a way." I am moving ahead despite the increasing obstacles that are presented to a mother and a wife. We fight against negative thinkers who want to cut off one's wings before they take flight. Now, I know that it is not too late and that if I struggle for something I can attain it.

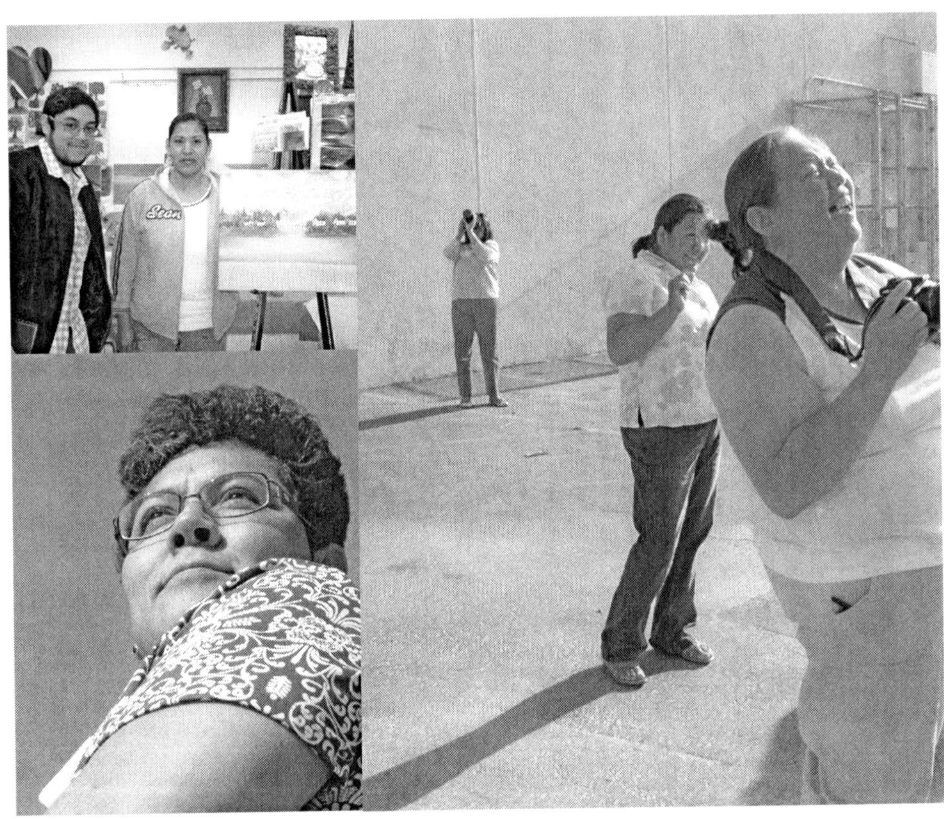

Siempre escuche la palabra querer es poder. Pero me decía eso es para otras personas y no para mi. Mi vida era esposo, hijos y una casa. Yo lamentaba no haber estudiado siendo joven y soltera. Pero un día la oportunidad toco a mi puerta con los nuevos directores en la escuela donde estudiara mi hijo y cambio mi vida haciendo me ver que la frase querer es poder, y la superación, es posible sin importar la edad. Estoy superando los obstáculos que como aumenten se representen a una madre y esposa. Luchamos en contra de personas de pensamiento negativo que quieren cortar las alas antes de que uno vuela. Ahora se que nunca es tarde, y si lucho por ello lo puedo lograr.

- MARIA MARTINEZ

I believe that when there is a will there is a way. My name Juan and I am unemployed and disabled. But that is not an excuse or obstacle to occupy my time in serving my community and to augment my knowledge, my spirit, and my faith. This [process] began as a volunteer 16 years ago. All that I feel and do is for the good of our children and for all students in general. As parents we want our children, and students, to feel confident and proud of us even though we are humble but capable of obtaining our goals.

Pienso que "querer es poder" y lo bueno cuesta un esfuerzo. Mi nombre es Juan y estoy desempleado y deshabilitado. Pero eso no es escusa ni obstáculo para ocupar mi tiempo en servir a la comunidad y a alimentar mi conocimiento, espíritu, y fe. Esto empezó como voluntario desde hace diez y seis años. Todo lo siento y hago por el bien de nuestros hijos y todos los estudiantes en general. Como padres queremos que nuestros hijos y alumnos sientan confianza y orgullo de nosotros aunque somos sencillos pero capaces de logar objetivos.

- JUAN MUNOZ

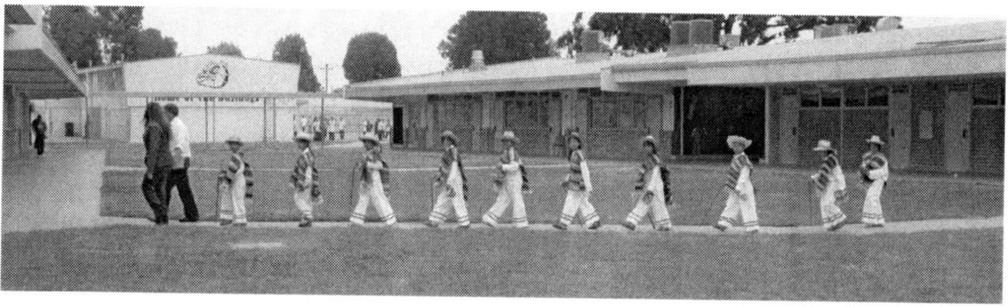

My name is Clara Muñoz and I represent Bunch Middle School. The school helped improve my self-esteem by attending the computer classes [graphic design]. This makes me feel good because I'm learning something different and I can help my children with their homework. And, in addition, through art I can express myself as a human being. Now that they have brought these UCLA [ArtsBridge] classes ... because I never imagined that the university would reach out to our school. As a parent, and mother of a family, I recommend that the schools function better with participation of parents, teachers, administrators and children.

Mi nombre es Clara Muñoz. Represento la escuela Bunche Middle School. La escuela me ha ayudado a mi autoestima. He mejorado al estar asistiendo las clases de computación [diseño gráfico]. Me hacen sentir bien porque estoy aprendiendo algo diferente y al que puedo ayudar a mis hijos con sus tareas. Y a través del arte me puedo expresar como ser humano y ahora que nos han traído estas clases de UCLA...porque nunca me imagine que la universidad se acercara nuestra escuela. Yo recomiendo como padre, o madre de familia, que las escuelas funcionan mejor con la participación de padres, maestros, administradores, y niños.

- CLARA MUNOZ

I am a dedicated and enterprising person with the internal strength to realize my dreams. As part of a community with the desire to improve ourselves, I have been given the strength to fight along with them shoulder to shoulder. [Just] as I have achieved my dreams, I hope that they realize theirs too. Being a woman, wife, mother, and daughter and also as part of this society, day by day, I feel a deeper obligation to and have developed a better understanding of those around me. Helping is a word filled with commitment that frightens many but it is just a simple word after all, that for me signifies the opening of ones heart and a continuation of helping others. For me it signifies love, working together and dedication to a cause. Reaching for and realizing the goals of all is part of what our family at Bunch Middle School in Compton does.

Soy emprendedora dedicaba y como tan fuerza interior que me ayuda conseguir mis sueños. El ser parte de una comunidad llena de deseos de superación me da la fuerza para luchar juntos a ellos hombro con hombro. Y así como yo he conseguido mis sueños espero que ellos logran los suyos. Ser mujer, esposa, madre, hija ya parte de esta sociedad me obligaba mas de mi cada día y también me ayuda a comprender a la gente de mi alrededor. Ayudar es una palabra llena de compromiso que a muchas personas espanta pero si a esta es simple y sencilla palabra me busca su significado de abrir a tu corazón y continuaras ayudando. Para mi significa amor y trabajo unión y dedicación. Alcanzando y realizando las metas de los demás eso es parte de la familia de Bunch Middle School en Compton.

- ALICIA PALAFOX

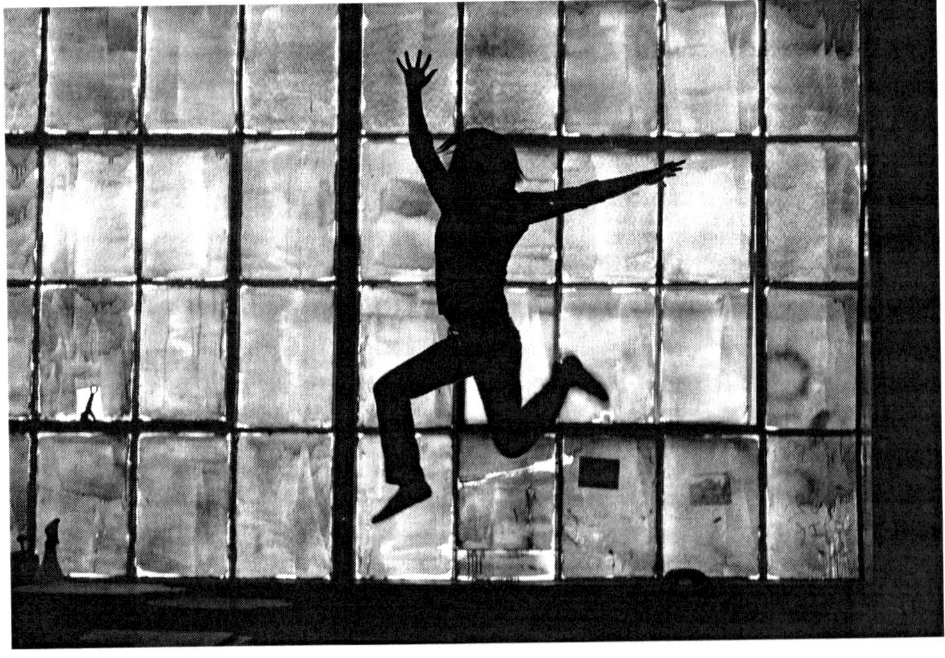

DRAMATIZING BORDERS
THROUGH THEATER ARTS

Amy Shimshon-Santo

Learning through the arts begins with the simple step of gaining literacy in the language of a specific art form, articulating and performing personal ideas and opinions, and building community by facilitating constructive critique, discussion, and participation that sparks personal and social change. Children's individual and household concerns can find outlets for expression through their creativity. The stories children tell can increase public awareness of the issues that impact their daily lives. One crucial concern for many children in Los Angeles is the personal and familial implications of U.S. immigration policy. In *Severing a Lifeline: The Neglect of Citizen Children in America's Immigration Enforcement Policy* (2009), the Urban Institute finds that:

> *Of the approximately 5 million children of undocumented immigrants residing in the United States, more than 3 million are U.S. citizens. Born here, these children derive their citizenship from the Fourteenth Amendment to the Constitution. Current immigration law and enforcement policy is marginalizing what it means for these children to be U.S. citizens. Increased interior immigration enforcement action by ICE, in the form of high-profile worksite raids and home raids, has resulted in the arrest, detention and deportation of record numbers of undocumented immigrants over the past several years. In the process, tens of thousands of children of undocumented immigrants, including citizen children, have seen their families torn apart, or experienced the effective deportation of the entire family to countries as foreign to them as they are to other American children (2009: 1).*

Immigration policy was an issue raised by students in Thomas Turner's class at George Washington Carver Middle School. This case provides an example of how youth can translate and transmit personal concerns to broader publics through theater.

An important synergy ensued when a group of students at George Washington Carver Middle School created and performed an original play called "Welcome to the Border Now Go Back Where You Came From." The play was developed with teaching artist Lee Sherman of the Center Theater Group in collaboration with Thomas Turner. Sherman used Brazilian dramaturge/activist Augusto Boal's Legislative Theater techniques to create the theater piece with youth.

Conquering their initial trepidations after weeks of rehearsal and study, the group performed their play to an enthusiastic audience in the school auditorium. The original play included a powerful tableau with a line of teenagers grasping arms to form an impenetrable wall of bodies that stretched the width of the auditorium. The youth wore block letters strung around their necks that spelled out the word b-o-r-d-e-r. The first time this tableau appeared in the play, it represented the geographic U.S. border. A young actor playing the role of an immigrant called out "Ayúdenme!" as they attempted to pry through the wall and cross over. "Está dificil!" the actors forming the wall replied in brash unison, their heads hanging down.

In a subsequent scene, the youth resurrected the border tableau again, to represent another border – the border to higher education. First, an actor playing the role of "undocumented student" moved successfully through primary and secondary school with high grades. "Congratulations!" the actor portraying the role of teachers said, as she received diplomas for excelling at each phase of her studies. But, after high school, the wall reappeared again on stage. "Ayúdenme!" the undocumented student called out as a placard reading "college" was held above the heads of the border tableau. As she tried unsuccessfully to cross the border into higher education the actors yelled back, "Está dificil!" while she struggled helplessly.

At the end of the play, the cast welcomed questions and answers from the audience. One classroom teacher asked the group, "Now that you have made a play about immigrant student rights, how will you change legislation for undocumented students?" A perplexing silence ensued. Was it enough to create an educational tool that drew attention to this important topic? How could they take their concerns a step farther? At this opportune moment I chose to perform my role as university professor audience member in a way that was more welcoming than a wall. I raised my hand and praised the students for their work and invited the young actors to UCLA to perform their play and to meet with student activists on campus who have been formative in changing legislation for undocumented students through Assembly Bill 540 (AB 540) and the Dream Act.

George Washington Carver Middle School, the Center Theater Group, and ArtsBridge collaborated to present the play at UCLA, welcomed the students to campus with a university tour, and held a roundtable discussion with student leaders about AB 540. Students, teachers, and administrators learned that undocumented students *can* indeed attend university in California and pay local tuition as a result of this legislation. However, because the Dream Act was not passed through the legislature, undocumented students still *cannot* receive sufficient public financial aid, nor get a driver's permit, nor hold a job requiring a social security card. In other words, currently undocumented students can prepare themselves for a career they are not yet permitted to work in. However, with diligent personal and social action, that, too, will change. As one audience member reminded the group, the United States was legally founded by a group of foreign born.

The positive impact of the collaboration was instantaneous and mutual. UCLA students (student activists and ArtsBridge Scholars) were pleased to meet teenagers who were asking the hard questions regarding educational access for undocumented youth. The teenagers were inspired by the struggles and activism of undocumented university students who overcame tremendous odds to pursue their dreams. Classroom teachers, teaching artists, and school administrators who were unaware of the AB 540 legislation learned about legal rights for undocumented students and will be more likely to better advise parents and future students about their options. Finally, the performance and roundtable made it clear to participants how social change happens – through consistent dedicated effort over time. Undocumented students have the right to an education, and it is a sign of civic responsibility to inform oneself and demand educational rights for all. These events and discussions, sparked by youth voice in theater, inspired participants to rededicate themselves to achieve educational justice for undocumented students through public action.

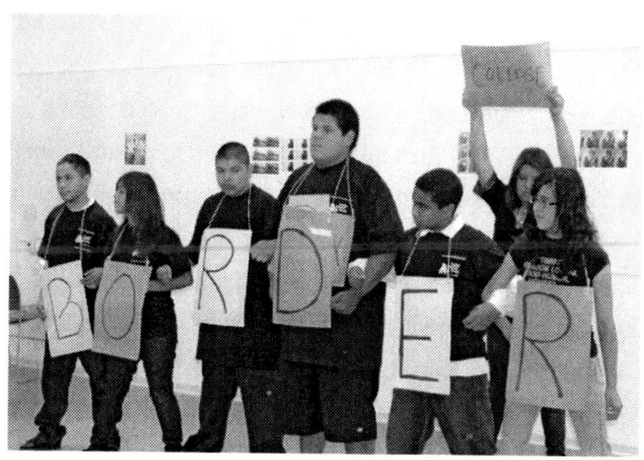

THE LANGUAGE OF CREATIVITY
MAKING SPACE FOR ARTISTIC INTELLIGENCES

Cynthia Wennstrom

This essay is a reflection of one of the most challenging and rewarding experiences of my undergraduate experience at UCLA. Many people – including my professors, mentors, peers, and students – made this experience possible. Without them, I would not have been able to take on this challenge, almost fail miserably, and pick myself up again…only to come out the other side enlightened that I had successfully contributed to something bigger than myself. More importantly, I had the opportunity to witness my students make rich connections through art, confirming a personal conviction that the arts are a tremendous force in a young person's life.

This article is the result of what I learned throughout my residency as a teaching artist at Millikan Middle School and a scholar in the ArtsBridge program at UCLA. Some of its content is taken almost directly from an oral presentation I gave at the "Reflection On Action: UCLA's Engagement with Urban Schools and Communities Symposium," held at the University of California Los Angeles on June 2, 2007.

As I sit here on the eve of my college graduation, I admit that I cannot keep from dusting off dozens of memories I've cherished throughout my young life as an undergraduate at one of the most prestigious public universities in the country. Lectures. Parties. Projects. Final exams. Art shows. Student demonstrations. One a.m. burrito runs. These are some of the usual memories a soon-to-be college alumna never forgets. Even more memorable to me are the people who helped shape me as the confident and intelligent young woman I am today, including my family, friends, fellow Art students, and professors. But when I review the most defining moments of my life, I keep rewinding past the last four years until I reach the fourth grade.

When I was ten years old my mother was inspired by an instinct she had that one day I would be an artist and a teacher, just like my grandfather had been when he was alive. She enrolled me in private art lessons that took place each week after school, and on the first day of class I had already convinced myself that I would never be an artist. Decked in headgear and my school jumper, I entered a small, white room filled with bottles of turpentine and boxes of oil paints that made my nose crinkle. Kids of all sizes were sitting at tall wooden easels and effortlessly reproducing paintings by masters of the Italian Renaissance. Everyone appeared to have the natural ability to draw and paint with watercolors, pencil, pastels, paints, and charcoal – while simultaneously having a great time. It was all so exciting, but I quickly reminded myself that I was not an artist. I had never felt so inept and scared than the day I entered this white room full of so many talented people.

An older woman who sensed my newness walked over to introduce herself. Her name was Athena, and she led me to a pile of pictures that consisted of birds, dogs, houses, fruit, and other simple subjects. According to my new teacher, I would be able to finish drawing any of these life-like pictures by the end of the day. Little beads of sweat dropped down my face as I realized that my stick-figure skills probably would not come in handy for this. After an awkward silence, I hastily decided that I would try drawing a picture of a little yellow duck. But as I stared at the blank piece of paper in front of me, nothing came out. No one had ever taught me how to be creative before – especially not in school. So I sat there, frozen, and afraid of being wrong.

Sensing my nerves, Athena assured me that to there was no wrong way to start a drawing. She said, "Draw what you see, not what you think you see." She opened a small box, took out a yellow pastel, placed it in my tiny hand, and showed me how to glide it across the paper. She taught me how to observe the different tones created by the light and how to convey subtleties in texture, while at the same time encouraging me to use my imagination. She showed me how to blend different layers of colors together, and then she would leave so that I could practice on my own. She would always come back every now and then to make little suggestions about how I could make my picture better, but she also made sure to tell me what I did well. After two and a half hours of instruction, an array of shapes and colors formed a beautiful duckling swimming in a little pond. Rich blues and purples juxtaposed against a red and orange sunset, golden strands of the setting sun glistened on a deep blue sea, and I was, in fact, an artist.

Athena will probably never know the impact she had on me that day – the last time that I ever doubted myself and also the first time that an intense curiosity burned inside of me. I learned how to look at my surroundings differently by training my eyes to focus on shapes, lines, tones and colors. Making art truly fascinated me. Throughout the following years of Art school, including my years at UCLA, I acquired various skills and habits that have contributed to my holistic education as an engaged and reflective human being: observation, expression, persistence, and reflection, among many others. More importantly, I have come to realize that these skills would not have been developed without a physical space that values this kind of creative thinking.

As I keep this memory in the back of my mind, I also imagine tomorrow's commencement and feeling of the degree that I worked so hard for in my hand. As the most important piece of paper I will have ever worked for up to this point in my life and a symbol of academic and artistic achievement, this degree will define me as an artist and validate my role as a cultural leader in society. But when I think about the status of arts education in today's K-12 schools, I almost second-guess the legitimacy of my own education. Where did all the art classes go?

There is much debate about what the Arts actually teach and why it is necessary for every child to have an Arts education, and there are many theories that either defend or criticize this notion. An important researcher and advocate for arts education, Howard Gardner developed the theory of multiple intelligences, which argues that a child's overall intelligence cannot be measured by traditional methods of instruction, because they treat every child's learning process the same (Gardner 1999). Instead, this theory advocates for the integration of student-centered instruction, whereby the eight different kinds of intelligences studied by Garner are fostered in each child, and whereby the natural abilities and strengths of each child are valued as an intelligence. Two of the eight intelligences that Gardner studied are related to the Arts: "visual-spatial" and "musical"; but despite this finding, "89% of California K-12 schools fail to offer a standards-based course of study in [...] music, visual arts, theatre, and dance" (Woodworth 2007:xiii).

If visual-spatial thinking and musical thinking are intelligences, why are California's children being denied access to their own intelligences by educators? Not startling is the fact that, according to SRI International's summary of key findings of arts education in California, students attending "high-poverty schools have less access to arts instruction than their peers in more affluent communities" (Woodworth 2007:xiii). Is it at all possible to consider the likelihood that space for the Arts in schools might be positively correlated with student success rates? If the goal of education in this country is to educate each child according to their needs for the purposes of equal opportunity, then unfortunately, we are failing. The little space that is left for our youth to be valued creatively speaks poorly of our public education system and our openness to new ideas about learning. Although one could argue that this is a result of lack of funding, it is also true that this results from the ideologies of a culture that refuses to recognize the important function of Art in local and global communities.

For the culmination of my senior ArtsBridge project at UCLA, I made a presentation entitled "Making Space for Artistic Intelligences," in light of this idea that public education has been progressively devaluing the physical and metaphorical space for creative thinking, which has led to a major decrease in arts education classes for many students. My presentation focused on my personal experiences working as an arts-educator-in-training at two public middle schools in Los Angeles, whose students I worked with were receiving arts instruction for the first time. In ten minutes, I tried to recapture all that I had learned during my residency that would advocate for more Arts in schools.

Over the course of five months I taught a standards-based fine art curriculum to 11 seventh and eighth grade students at Millikan Middle School in Sherman Oaks, California. I was teamed up with their English teacher, Ms. Betty Poncin, who was as enthusiastic as I was about bringing Art into the classroom. I learned that her students were part of the Directed Reading and Writing Program, a class that gave support to students who struggled to perform in their reading and writing classes, and thus, had low test scores. I also learned that, although Millikan Middle School is an arts magnet, students in the Directed Reading and Writing Program were receiving double the amount of English instruction as everybody else. As a result, they were being denied any Arts electives, with the expectation that they would focus more on core subjects and improve their performance on state tests.

If visual-spatial thinking and musical thinking are intelligences, why are California's children being denied access to their own intelligences by educators? Not startling is the fact that, according to SRI International's summary of key findings of Arts education in California, students attending "high-poverty schools have less access to arts instruction than their peers in more affluent communities" (Woodworth 2007:xiii). Is it at all possible to consider the likelihood that space for the Arts in schools might be positively correlated with student success rates? If the goal of education in this country is to educate each child according to his or her needs for the purposes of equal opportunity, then unfortunately, we are failing. The little space that is left for our youth to be valued creatively speaks poorly of our public education system and our openness to new ideas about learning. Although one could argue that this is a result of lack of funding, it is also true that this results from the ideologies of a culture that refuses to recognize the important function of art in local and global communities.

Since the 2001 No Child Left Behind Act, test scores have been a determining factor for the distribution of federal funding for public schools, which motivates school administrators and educators to focus on core subject areas such as reading and math. What this means for the Arts is catastrophic; they are progressively being cut from schools, sometimes for the mere sake of receiving federal funding. SRI International concludes that the "pressure to improve test scores in other content areas is another top barrier to arts education" (Woodworth 2007:xiii).

It is interesting to argue that taking away Arts instruction is purported to strengthen a weakness in another subject, such as English, when there are actually many overlapping concepts and thought processes, including composition, expression, and originality. For example, one common free-writing exercise for students in an English composition class is to describe the setting of a story or narrative through their senses, such as how a place sounds or smells. Although this exercise promotes creativity, certain students are turned off by the written word and cannot think through the written word. I realized that in order for some students to be expressive in their writing, they would need a means to express their senses in a more visceral way. I decided that one of our first projects would be an investigation of the senses through collage art – a very tangible and physical means of expression. I wondered if perhaps the students would be able to enter their writing tasks with more freedom and confidence after having the opportunity to describe through materiality.

We examined the works of two famous collage artists, Kurt Schwitters and Robert Rauschenberg, who played with the materiality of paint and other objects. The students were inspired by the range of materials – such as paint, plastic, magazine clippings, trash, and wood – that these artists used to create such stunning and sensory works. I passed around five "sensory boxes," and each contained a smell, sound or taste that the students would have to describe using collage. Incorporating the design principles applied by Schwitters and Rauschenberg, the students designed their own sensory collages, which were truly physical manifestations of the idea of sensory imagery.

The concepts of design – including composition, color, and contrast – are all valuable elements in language arts. One student created an explosive composition of paint and materials and chose specific images that would suggest the feeling of soft, fluffy blankets or newly laundered clothes. In the vein of Rauschenberg, she also radically juxtaposed her soft images with one harsh stroke of red paint that cut across her otherwise soft composition. This decision gave the piece a very intelligent sense of tension and helped her understand the idea of contrast in her writing. The students were thus able to explore abstract concepts by learning concrete principles of design, which they will be able to translate into their writing skills. In no way did this project debilitate the students' performance in other content areas; in fact, I would argue that Arts instruction only added to their success in other subject areas.

Although Art can help students better understand concepts in other subjects, Art should also be valued as a subject of its own accord, with its own benefits to the emotional and spiritual growth of an individual. Several students made rich connections between their personal lives and one of the first class projects, an improvisational composition based on the 20th century abstract expressionist, Wassily Kandinsky, who created paintings based on music. First, I introduced the students to the idea of improvisation by giving them strips of different colored paper in increments of thirty seconds, with which they were to quickly arrange onto a piece of paper. Next, I instructed them to find their own rhythm by arranging the strips of paper in order to convey an emotion they were feeling that day.

One particular student, Jasmine Hardaway, was so deeply entranced by her own artwork that she felt compelled to give an oral reflection of her work in front of the entire class. According to Jasmine, she associated the strips of paper with the wings of birds, and she associated birds with the feeling she gets from singing. She explained that singing made her feel as free as a bird flying in the air, so she chose to arrange the bird-like strips of paper in a way that suggested that they were flying off the edge of the paper. Finally, she was so moved by her own art that she sang one of her church songs for the whole class to hear.

Jasmine's ability to communicate visually and musically, just as Wassily Kandinsky had done in his famous paintings, was a testament to her visual-spatial and musical intelligence, as well as her ability to make meaningful and rich connections between her art and her life. Her experience exemplified the powerful connections and advantages that arts education gives students who are struggling to perform in their regular classes, by granting them access to other kinds of thinking in which they are more fluent. Unfortunately, many students share Jasmine's situation because they are underperforming in core subject areas and subsequently, are being denied access to classes other than English, history, math, and science. But as a witness to the excellence exhibited by Jasmine and the other students in my class, I am convinced that these are the students who actually need the Arts.

The last project, entitled "Re-Packaging Identity," captured the students' individual and cultural identities. The students made collages out of small canvases, which represented their lives through photomontage, paint, and other materials. We focused on the African-American experience in the 20th and 21st centuries as depicted by three different black artists – Renee Cox, Romare Bearden, and Kerry James Marshall – which exposed the students for the first time to art as social commentary. We investigated the ways in which Cox exaggerated and contorted the features and colors of African-American faces through photography, in order to question racial stereotypes associated with people of color, particularly blacks. The other two artists we studied portrayed the places they lived in as signifiers for their own personal and cultural identities. We surveyed Bearden's collages, which portrayed life during the African-American cultural revolution within the Harlem Renaissance. We also looked at Marshall's collages, which depicted his identity as a young black youth growing up during the Los Angeles rebellion in Watts, California.

The students studied and applied the principles of design incorporated by these three artists, and they created amazing objects that were visually stimulating and relevant to their different experiences as diverse youth with growing identities. On the back of the canvas, the students recreated their own portraits in the vein of Renee Cox, by cutting up mirrored images of their faces and creating a face photomontage. On the front of the canvas, using Bearden and Marshall as inspiration, they manipulated different textured paper, paint, and magazine clippings to illustrate the different neighborhoods they come from. One student, Gladys Alvarez, made very perceptive connections to the cultural and artistic relevancy of the project by creating a realistic portrayal of the housing community that she lived in. She fabricated original images for her collage from scratch by incorporating small bits of magazine clippings and positioning them together – a technique she learned from Romare Bearden.

Not only were the students successful at artistic expression, but also at the reflection on the social significance of art. The students questioned the idea of representation in today's society, especially the stereotypes associated with African-American culture. As we looked at Kerry James Marshall's famous depictions of Watts during the civil rights movement, a discussion ensued about the students' various perspectives of Los Angeles. The students, who recognized the setting of Watts in Marshall's paintings, shared their experiences as natives of that part of the city with other students. The others listened with curiosity and open minds as they learned new perspectives about the city in which they lived. The discussion was a wonderful cultural exchange that resulted in a very thoughtful and profound lesson on the differences in the urban landscape of Los Angeles.

This project was a success as a result of the expressive, analytical, and reflective skills that the students gained. They questioned and investigated their own identities, while learning about the identities of other students in their class. They learned that what one looks like and where one lives are agents of representation that have a deep effect on our perception of history, our perceptions of others, and our perception of ourselves. These perceptions led to the question: "Do we accurately represent the identities which we show to people, or are we something more than what our 'packages' tell people we are?"

The art class finally ended with a field trip to the Hammer Museum. It was a wonderful culminating experience in which the students enjoyed the fruits of their labor and applied what they had learned in class to the artworks of nationally and internationally known artists from Los Angeles. We saw the exhibit, Eden's Edge, where I witnessed some of the most thoughtful connections I could ever hope for in my students. In one particular instance, we were walking through Ginny Bishton's collages of abstract organic shapes, which were comprised of deconstructed photographs of plants and flowers. One student exclaimed, "I know how they did this," and proceeded by explaining to the class and our tour guide the process of collage art. In another instance, two of my students fell ten minutes behind the tour guide, because they were busy discussing a sculpture by artist, Matthew Monahan. Their interest in the processes of art was incredible.

As my ArtsBridge residency at Millikan Middle School finally came to a close, I left with the feeling that this was just the beginning of my experience as an arts advocate. As a firsthand witness to the rich and meaningful connections that the students in Ms. Poncin's class made through the Arts, I was convinced of the immediate and long-term benefits of having space for the Arts in schools. By giving the students ample space to grow creatively, they expanded their knowledge of artistic processes, cultural differences, personal identities, and even concepts, that could be applicable to their writing. Students learned perceptive and creative skills and began to understand large, abstract concepts. From consumers they turned into cultural producers. They created community by sharing stories of cultural diversity. They learned what it means to be a reflective citizen of the world, and they enjoyed school. I could not have asked for more.

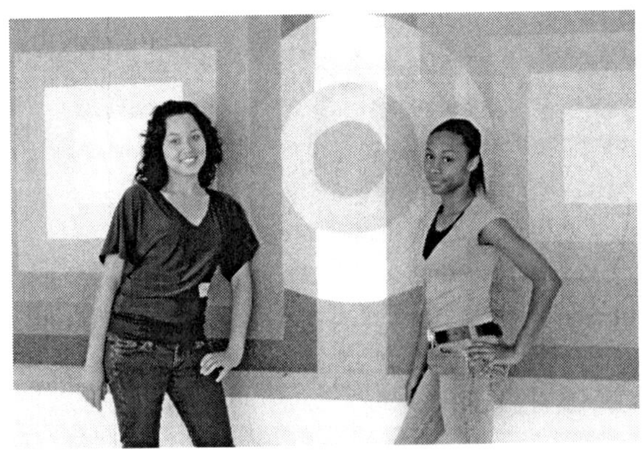

MY VOICE CAN FLY

Interview with Alicia Paniagua & Amy Shimshon-Santo

Amy: Alicia, can you tell me what salsa dancing means to you?

Alicia: To me salsa dancing means a way to explore culture and communication through your body. It is a way to make yourself feel better about your body and how it moves…

Amy: As you are finishing up your last class of your undergraduate career, how has the experience of teaching salsa touched on interests you might like to pursue?

Alicia: All along I knew that I loved to dance, but I didn't know how to put dance into my education. Obviously, I was of that misconception that education and dance can't be bridged, but through this I learned that it can – and very much so!

Amy: How did the ArtsBridge courses differ from the other classes that you took as an undergraduate at UCLA?

Alicia: Right off the bat, here you actually get to go out into the community and put your work into practice while other classes…it was kind of dry after awhile because you are just sitting behind a lecturer and you go in and regurgitate what they tell you pretty much. But, this (teaching salsa to youth) every time you go in it is something different…You learn a lot about yourself. You learn a lot about the community, and the community has a lot to offer that one person coming in… Just going out and experiencing what is was like to teach, to be placed in those environments where kids are not looked at as dancers or artists, whatever the reasoning may be, and be that person that inspires them to say "Oh, I can actually do this!" That was something amazing.

Amy: You were working with an ELL classroom. What did it mean to you to work with a group of kids that started off in Spanish and then were gaining their English skills?

Alicia: It means a lot because I did come here when I was 8 years old and I didn't know any English. Luckily, I wasn't placed in an ESL class because I was able to pick up the language, but I can see that to these kids it meant a lot to have a person that they could actually relate to. Just to say, "Oh, you are from El Salvador?" or "You weren't born here?" and look at you and you are in college … Just [me] being there was something very motivating for them I believe. They were very impressed and wanting to learn and wanting to ask me "Why did I want to continue to work with the school?" Some of them probably expressed an interest when they had never thought about going to college. They would say, "Do you really think I could go?" and I would say, "Yeah, you could *really* go if you *really* want to. You can do anything you want to do."

Amy: That's great. I saw that you made bilingual handouts of important icons in salsa history for your class. Can you describe the work you did using Celia Cruz?

Alicia: I brought one of her songs in as a way to introduce the kids to salsa music and lyrics. What revolutionary or better image than Celia Cruz? Not only in Latin America but also in the states. Everyone knows her face or her contributions to music. So, I brought in a picture and we read over the lyrics of the song. The song sparked interest in a lot of the kids because it has the rhythm of the "I Will Survive" song in English.

Amy: What are some of the words you were experimenting with in the song?

Alicia: One of the main phrases that we talked about was *"Mi voz puede volar y puede atravesar."* So, we talked about "How can your voice fly?," or "How can our voices pass through?" Why would she [Celia Cruz] mention this specific term with the voice and flying? We talked about how she is from Cuba, but her music is heard all over the world. So, there is a correlation between how her voice flew, and her message flew, and her songs became popular all over the world. She was able to be heard all over the world.

Amy: Does this have a special message for people who have immigrated to the U. S.?

Alicia: I believe so. When the kids wrote their responses they talked how her voice correlated with being free, or attaining something greater than they ever imagined.

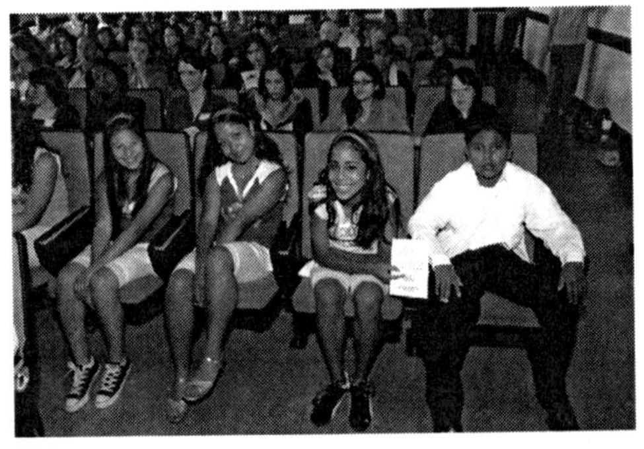

MEDIA LITERACY IN MIDDLE SCHOOL
VISUALIZING A PERSONAL POINT OF VIEW

Lisa Nuñez

In history class, teaching is often just from a textbook and primary source documents, and students don't often get a chance to express themselves in a creative way. It was great to have this ritual every week to be able to do something a little bit out of the norm. My students got a lot out of the experience.

The first thing that I noticed is that every week my students did a current events homework assignment where they read a news article, they broke it down, and they had the express themselves in a written form. In this case, my students had the chance to express their point of view visually. For some of them, that was easy, but for some of them, that was a challenge. It was something that they weren't used to doing. They get so many hours of practice every week expressing themselves in their English classes through writing, but it's not very often that we ask them to express these same arguments visually.

The second thing is that at the very end, when the students had the chance to put their work up and engage in critique it was interesting to gage and see their reaction to their piece up on the wall because it's very different on the wall from the computer screen, and then to see other people's reactions to it. The kids were surprised…I thought it was great for them to be able to step back from their work, look at it, and have others respond to it. Sometimes their opinions came across very clearly, and sometimes their images were interpreted by the audience differently than they had intended. To see them go through that experience was very rewarding.

It was great for my students to be producers of media rather than just consumers of media. I asked them every week to read something out of a newspaper, and now they had a chance to actually produce something, to influence other people, and to get other people's responses to it. I think it is important that students can see that every piece of media is essentially produced by a person, or a group of people, and that their point of view, and what they have to say about it, is just as valid as what anybody else has to say about the issue.

DISCOVERING LANGUAGE ASSETS THROUGH DESIGN

Laurel Bybee

We are born to create; each and every one of us has creative energy. This energy is precious and should never be stifled. Unfortunately, for students who have been categorized as *English Language Learners* (ELL), the opportunities for artistic expression in school are few and far between. A double blocking of students in two English classes is often mandated, making them unable to participate in and enjoy an arts elective. As educators, we must take responsibility to make connections between this standard curriculum and the arts, in order to engage more students. As Rabkin states, "Where we blend academic disciplines and the arts, we restore the worldliness and cogency of the disciplines" (Rabkin 2004:62).

During my fourteen-week residency at Millikan, I attempted to bring graphic design, a communicative art form, into the classroom in order to creatively engage more students in learning English. I was inspired by Beverly Tatum's ABC approach to teaching. The ABC approach seeks to affirm identities, build up the community, and cultivate a sense of leadership. One problem with how the "English Language Learning" designation is conceptualized is that it fails to affirm the student's bilingualism as an asset. Their native language is seen as an obstacle that has to be overcome, and this creates an invisibility and marginality that will ultimately undermine their success in school. It is important that we help all students affirm their identities with the ultimate goal of sharing their success with peers. Thus, with each project, my lesson plans were tailored around their lives, their language, and their daily activities, in an attempt to affirm their own history and experiences. In the final project students were asked to create a statement about their personalities in both English and the language they speak at home. They were given the freedom of self-expression, which became apparent in their self-reflective final posters.

Building a sense of community within the classroom is very important. It is the 'B' in Tatum's ABC theory for teaching. It is difficult to build a sense of community while working in a computer lab. Every student is confined to their own environment within their personal computer. Most of the time design is a solitary practice, but there is no reason why design education should be void of community. In class, I hoped to foster a sense of sharing knowledge. For example, in a complex design program like Adobe Illustrator, it could take 15 minutes to find a certain function. This was important, considering that there were only two instructors for a class of 25 students. The exchange of knowledge often led to imitation, but it also fostered a sense of community within the classroom. When it came time to use the Canon Digital SLR's for our photo shoot, I paired up the students, who took turns sharing the roles of photographer and model. While the SLR camera may have been overwhelming for an individual student to tackle, I hoped that, as a pair, they would feel more confident to experiment when shooting for the final poster assignment. By utilizing photographic techniques such as framing and cropping, my students were cognizant of certain backgrounds and props that aided them in conveying their messages on a poster. The results of this communal exercise were amazing. Denis Novis was photographed in mid air, jumping above a horizon that is tilted from the skewed camera angle. There is so much life and energy in this pose that could not have been captured if I, or another teacher, was behind this camera. He would not convey the same exuberance, because there would be more pressure to conform or act a certain way.

Another activity that cultivated this sense of community was designing their family trees. Students were asked to go home and obtain information from their parents about their family's roots. Not only were the students asked to find names of their family, they were also asked to find their locations of birth. I hoped that this would prompt a dialogue with their families about where they came from. Perhaps they would do some research on specific locations to incorporate into the font or color choice. Kevin Diaz created a family tree with thick gothic lettering and a background of the Mexican flag. This pride about where we come from helps to emphasize that community is a significant part of our development. It is important that these students find a personal connection to their work.

The last step in Tatum's ABC's of education includes cultivating leadership. During class, I tried to start a dialogue about various examples of graphic design. I hoped that the students would show some leadership by expressing their opinions. Arriving at this stage was difficult. The dialogue, or more specifically, critique, is a necessary step in self-reflection and improving future work[1]. As designers, we learn, grow, discover, interpolate, communicate and critique in every assignment completed. With each addition to our portfolio of work, we can define a stage of growth. Toward the end of the residency, after the students had three solid projects under their belts, they were more apt and eager to start a dialogue about each other's work. Work was described in the most basic terms. At this stage, it was difficult for the students to move past just why they liked a certain color or font. If I had more time, I would have worked on developing a proper dialogue. However, during the last phase of the residency, the students proudly hung their work for the school in a converted dance space. They had the chance to share everything they had learned. It was gratifying to see some of the more outspoken students express their opinions in front of more than 40 other students; it showed courage and true leadership skills.

Moving beyond the basics of the art form occurred only after the students felt comfortable navigating Adobe Illustrator, which was a new learning environment for them. It took four weeks before the students could open a document, find the necessary tools and translate their vision onto the page. It is important to remember that most of these students do not have access to computers, let alone advanced computer graphics software. There was much difficulty grasping the idea that the icons in the tool palette aid in completing a very specific task. The students are so used to using the arrow for two things: clicking hyper links from myspace.com page or writing the occasional English essay. The concept that a curser can be used to create a graphic was a new frontier. While it was necessary to teach the program and the functions of these tools, I was cautious not to make the class into a tutorial session about Illustrator. If this were the case, the students would not be learning the fundamentals of design; they would be creating work that would soon look very dated. As designers we must remember not to rely on the tools or techniques to communicate the vision. Developing a solid visual process, where we define how we go about solving visual problems, helps us rely less on the computer program and more on our own curiosity, solutions and ingenuity. I assigned projects that would challenge the students both visually and intellectually.

Inspired by the maps of Lewis and Clark, Phase Two of the residency focused on map making. I spoke about the new frontiers that Lewis and Clark had come across in their travels, which I tried to connect with the frontiers of learning a new program like Illustrator. The classroom teacher I worked with would later make more connections during her lesson on Lewis and Clark. To reflect on their own travels, I asked the students to close their eyes and visualize the path they take every day from home to school. I wanted them to visualize the time and the space as they imagined this familiar journey. This route is so familiar that we can imagine every turn and stop necessary to arrive at our destination. Thus, the students were able to create these intricate maps. I call this a "visual information recall strategy" to aid in envisioning space and time relationship. This exercise is important because artists must learn to visualize a scene before it is created. The skill of perceiving and translating depth, space, and time into a static two-dimensional plane is beneficial for a variety of disciplines. This skill helps students to consciously move through new and unfamiliar environments, namely new frontiers. With this assignment, I was able to teach to the standards of "Artistic Perception," [2] linking this with a historical context and creating connections and relationships within their own lives. Creating lesson plans helped me to be more conscious of my own strengths and weaknesses as an educator and designer. While teaching, it was necessary to envision myself in that vulnerable learning stage. It was difficult to condense everything I had learned in graphic design in order to teach. I would relearn the fundamental elements of design that have become inherent in my practice. Through this experience I have grown into a stronger person who feels better equipped to lead a group of students. Most importantly, I hope to emphasize that everyone is creative, and creativity helps us learn. It is unfortunate that K-12 students designated as ELL are regularly denied the opportunity for an art elective. Further development of their own creative process will aid learning, discovery, and problem solving when arriving at new frontiers of education.

Notes

1   *The process of critique is an important skill for all artists to improve their work. This includes creating constructive criticism about other artists work as well as self criticism.*

2   *Artistic Perception as described in the State Standards where "Students effectively describe and analyze artistic choices in their own works, and works of others, using academic language and terminology most of the time with minimal assistance. Students effectively and with minimal prompts describe the influence of personal experience on the interpretation of artistic works. Students, with limited assistance, effectively develop and apply appropriate criteria for evaluating quality and effectiveness of artistic works."*

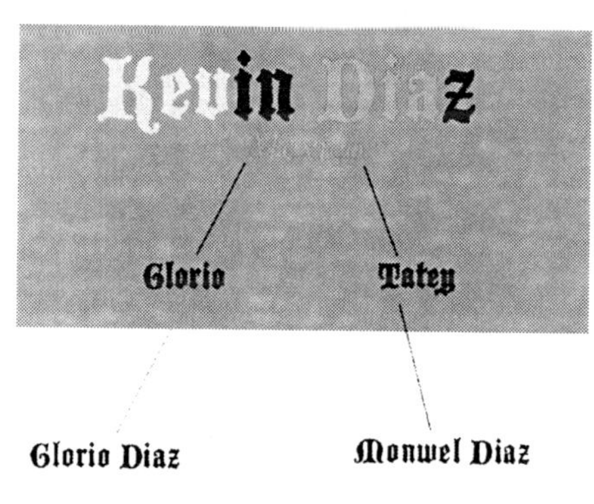

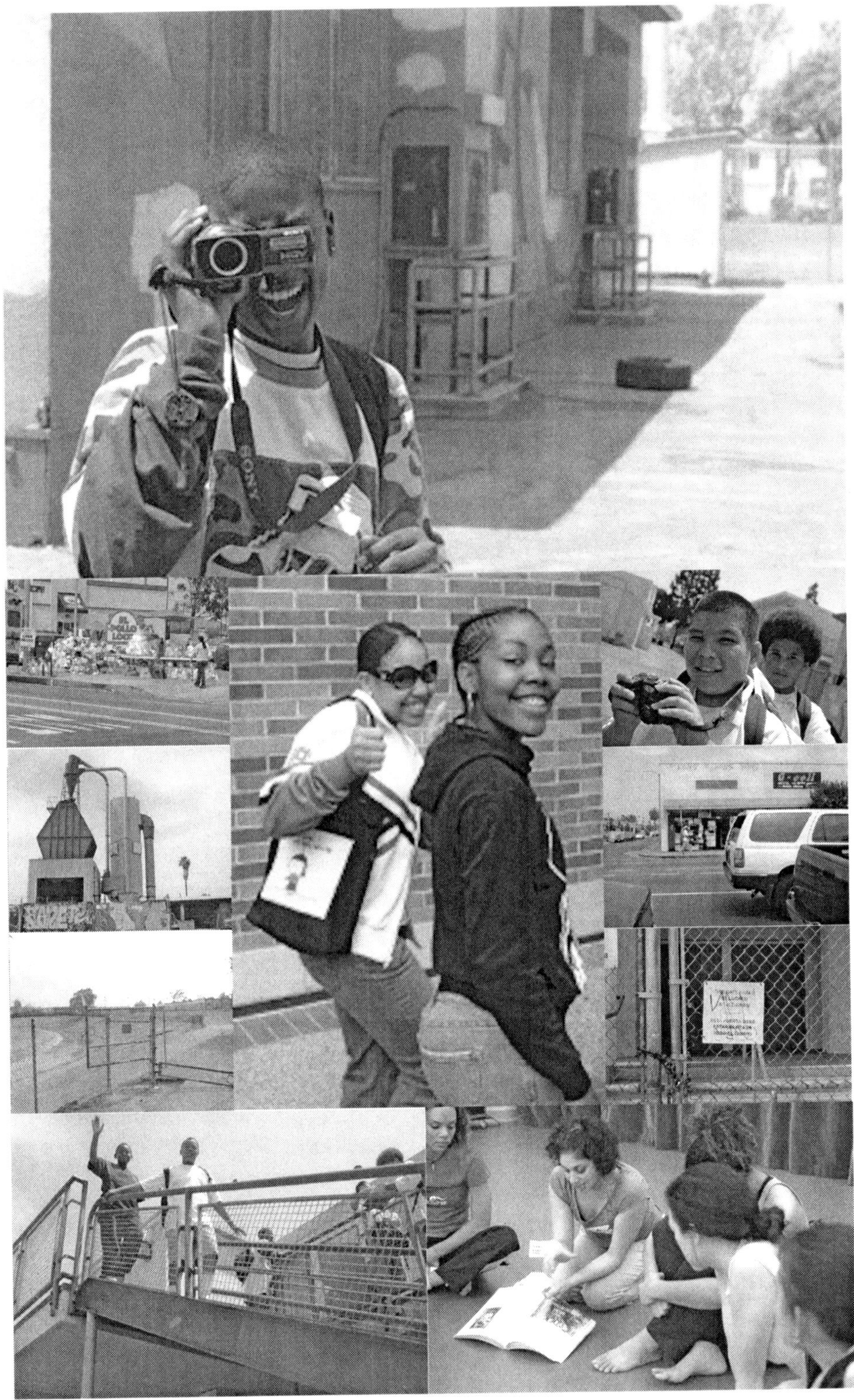

ARTS EDUCATION AS INQUIRY

Correlate Section Overview

For most arts educators it is a luxury to find time to write and reflect on a past teaching experience, because they are quickly jettisoned off to the next school project. As a nomadic arts educator, I may have spent as much time driving from school to school as I did in the classroom. This exposed me to the city in ways that most residents rarely see, and I became well versed in the expansive and disjointed geographies of Los Angeles County. I simply filed away that invaluable knowledge as "experience" and did not have the opportunity to reflect on it through critical writing. Years later, I make a point of encouraging reflection and analysis from my student arts teachers. Dancers, musicians, visual artists, and designers don't often think of themselves as community based researchers, but do as much fieldwork as an anthropologist, sociologist, or urban planner.

This section compiles analytical essays from arts instruction in dance, design, music, theater, video, and cultural studies. The authors make sense of what they taught and learned, explain their creative choices, and extract personal meaning from the teaching experience. In some cases, the writers propose public policy recommendations based on their analyses.

In an effort to address the exclusion of African American and Latino composers from public school music education curriculum, Tanitra Flenaugh created and taught a tango infused music curriculum for small ensembles at Bret Harte Middle School in South Los Angeles. Her essay, "Music, Freedom, and Tango," analyzes the importance of cultural relevance in primary and secondary music education. "Bringing Literature to Life Through Theater and Film," an essay by Iliana Phirripidis, describes how she and her colleague Jena McRae, and Guiding Teacher Kori Hamilton, used the arts as a vehicle for critical pedagogy at David Starr Jordan High School in Watts. From MacBeth MiniMovies to character analysis and scene development, their inventive literature infused theater and film curriculum that allowed students to engage with Shakespeare, Bradbury, and Esquivel on a personal level. Writing from an elementary school classroom, Lindsay Lindberg explains how she synthesized her interests in dance and physical therapy in "Storytelling, Dance, and Human Anatomy." "Dancing for Health" consolidates Norlyn Asprec's views about dance education as a useful intervention to prevent childhood obesity. Through fieldwork in South Los Angeles and Washington D.C., Asprec found that children in Los Angeles's low income neighborhoods are at higher risk for obesity due to limited healthy food choices and unsafe streets. To address this issue, she developed and taught a dance and nutrition curriculum at George Washington Carver Middle School and analyzed the importance of preventive health and coordination at the local, state, and federal levels. For Asprec, community activism and public policy are crucial to reducing childhood obesity, and dance education provides a positive alternative for physical exercise and cultural affirmation.

These analytical essays epitomize the aims of praxis-oriented research that links thought, analysis, and informed action. In this case, every researcher you will read is an artist, and each artist an educator.

MUSIC, FREEDOM, AND TANGO:
CULTURAL RELEVANCE IN MUSIC EDUCATION

Tantira Flenaugh

"To me freedom means being able to be who you want to be," stated Norma Ramirez, Bret Harte Preparatory Middle School (BHPMS) eighth grader. This personal realization was one of the central hopes behind my choice to explore the music of Argentine composer and bandoneón[1] player, Astor Piazzolla, with a group of 11 middle school students at Bret Harte Middle School in South Los Angeles. These seventh and eighth graders (ages 11-13) were at that critical age where they were forging their own identities. This was evident in their dress, in their spoken language, and, of course, in the music to which they listened voluntarily.

Within the United States' public school system, music programs often operate at a severe disadvantage, in which they are viewed as an abstract standalone, largely confined to learning instruments or learning to sing. Even after eighteen years of playing music, it was not until I was a graduate student that I had the opportunity to perform music from my ancestral background in a symphonic setting. For African Americans and Latinos in symphonic music this sad fact is quite common. Our diverse cultural contributions are often omitted from music education curriculum for children and adults. Not only is the music played important, but so, too, this inclusion of culturally diverse music educators. As an African American musician and educator I want to expose my students to high quality diverse composers from Latin America, the African Diaspora, and beyond to stop the practice of cultural exclusion and invisibility in symphonic music education.

My intention in teaching the life and music of Piazzolla was to show how music is one of the most integral aspects of human life - that it forms a seminal part of the cultural negotiations in which we are constantly engaged. Music can function as a reflection and expression of our views, struggles, and dreams. My belief was that if I could convincingly illuminate how we instinctually strive to discover our selfhood, my students would be drawn into both the music and issues of their own identity.

My group, the Bret Harte Chamber Woodwind Ensemble, consisted largely of Latino and two African-American students. There were three clarinetists, two flutists, two alto saxophonists, one tenor saxophonist, one trombonist and two percussionists. Each student already had one to two years of school band experience. Over the course of 15 weeks, my intent was to balance the demands of creating an unflappable musical ensemble while showing the students the ways in which Piazzolla negotiated his identity in his world.

Achieving the goals of the residency was complex; in spite of their experience, none of my students possessed any knowledge of either Piazzolla or the tango. The complexity arose in creating an enjoyable, rewarding, and concise program which would guide the students through obtaining the necessary knowledge and experience to perform at the culminating event. During our first session together, I talked about my personal and professional background, ArtsBridge[2], and asked the students to share something culturally interesting about their families. For example, one student shared with me the many types of dances her aunts have taught her, such as samba and salsa. The other students listened with interest. I then played for the students various examples of Latin American music, including folk, popular, and art music. In subsequent lessons, I focused on the history and music of Argentina. We started with the roots of tango and the social, political, and cultural aspects that molded this music, which in turn prepared us for our primary focus on Piazzolla and his creation Nuevo Tango. With this background knowledge, the students were able to obtain a deeper understanding of the music.

Though well trained by their school Band Director, Gregory Martin, in their first year or two I discovered that the students needed more grounding in rhythm, technical fluency on their instruments, and intonation. As a result, I made the strategic decision in Week Three to focus on a single major work - Piazzolla's *Libertango* - and the rich history surrounding it. In this way, the students discovered intimate knowledge about a particular region of the world, the musical characteristics of Nuevo tango, and a deeper awareness of self and the world. My work with the students focused on the following: the differences between small and large ensemble performance, the effects of cultural relevance, student reaction to performing the music, and the political dimensions of popular and symphonic music's interactions.

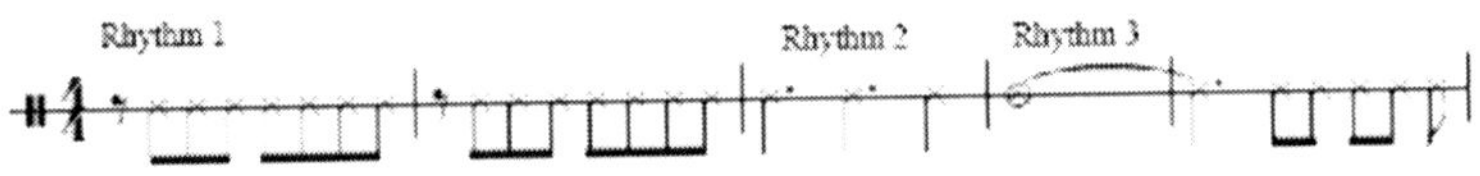

Example of the three main rhythms in Libertango

With most popular music, the internalization of the beat is imperative to express the music convincingly. Using the rhythm card and mimicking method, I got the students accustomed to listening with their ears, eyes, and bodies. I turned on the recording and without speaking motioned for them to look, listen, and copy my movements. I started tapping my heels on each beat of the music and waited for them to join me. Before clapping to each of the three rhythms, I first signaled for the students to listen; second, they clapped to the rhythm after me; and, third, I showed them an oversized card that represented that particular rhythm in musical notation. To reinforce their knowledge, I held up one rhythm card at a time for them to clap what they saw. These tools turned out to be highly effective.

Over the course of the residency I taught them the basic history of Piazolla and the musical characteristics of his music. For example, they learned that Piazzolla was a composer of both symphonic and tango music. He also was a prodigy bandoneonist who played everything from Mozart to popular music on his uniquely Argentinean instrument. The form of tango he created - Nuevo Tango - included inspirations ranging from Gerri Mulligan to Bach and Puccini[3].

The jazz elements in *Libertango* are apparent through the walking bass line, improvisation, and swing elements. In Piazzolla's recording, the string bass carries the bass line. The bass serves the same function in straightforward jazz music as it does in Nuevo Tango – it provides the glue for the song and sets the mood by establishing the groove and harmonic structure. Piazzolla also facilitates another important jazz element, improvisation. By repeating the beginning section, he allows the performers to invent variations on the melody. As in many jazz compositions, the pianist's left hand - often in bass clef - doubles the string bass as well. Piazzolla created his own "Piazzolla Swing." Although subtle, with enough experimentation my students were able to genuinely "swing."

My original curriculum included a unit on music arranging. However, upon contacting and meeting with different schools, I realized this would require a different approach so I put aside the arranging component. Ultimately my curriculum became a self-taught exercise on music arranging. I located the piano score for *Libertango* but the original instrumentation of the group included clarinet, flute, tenor saxophone, alto saxophone; trumpet, electric bass, trombone, and percussion. In order to get all of the instrumentalists to the same place in the music, I wrote out the three main phrases in three keys so that everyone could learn these phrases concurrently. This approach offered additional benefits, because it gave me an idea of which instrument or instrumentalist sounded best playing each phrase. Once the group was solidified and most of the students learned 80% of the music, I wrote an individual part for each player that accentuated their strong points in the music. In order to encourage cross listening and confidence, even while each student had a slightly different part from his or her neighbor, I reiterated in every rehearsal that, "Someone, somewhere, is playing your part!" Once they made the initial breakthrough, they found cross-listening a great source of security.

As the students became increasingly familiar with the music, I added on a new section - the B-section - to *Libertango*. One day Mayra Ontiveros said to me, "Hey Ms. Flenaugh, there's not any dynamics in this music!" My response was, "Good point Mayra. Let's come up with some." In music, dynamics refers to the variance of the volume of a note or tone. Just as in speech, dynamics are important in music, because it is vital for communicating the entire emotional range. Minus dynamics, music can sound monotonous and stifling. Many young band students just blow all the time at full volume. My student's inquiry into dynamics was remarkable for a number of reasons. First was the student's eagerness for a more encompassing interpretation of the music. Even though they were playing the notes with relative accuracy, the musicians wanted to extract the full spirit of Nuevo Tango. Instead of just telling them where to play louder or softer, I told them that we would work together to derive the dynamics for the whole piece. In this way they were able to exercise cooperative learning through guided discussion. They expressed their own creativity by deriving their own dynamics.

They also deepened their musical understanding by embracing other stylistic challenges in *Libertango*. Upon listening to the recording, they realized that the musicians played the song in a certain manner to create a jazzy dance feeling in the music. The students began to hear how the musicians on the recording played some notes shorter or longer, which contributed greatly to the stylistic sense of the music (even though it was not directly notated this way). This helped them understand their parts and my score as a roadmap rather than a polished interpretation. Through their developing musical awareness, they were able to deduce the articulation—a combination of shorter and longer notes—in order to capture the Piazzolla swing on the eight-note figure. By the day of the performance, the budding musicians were able to recreate Nuevo Tango at multifarious levels they had been entirely unaware of at the beginning of the 15 weeks.

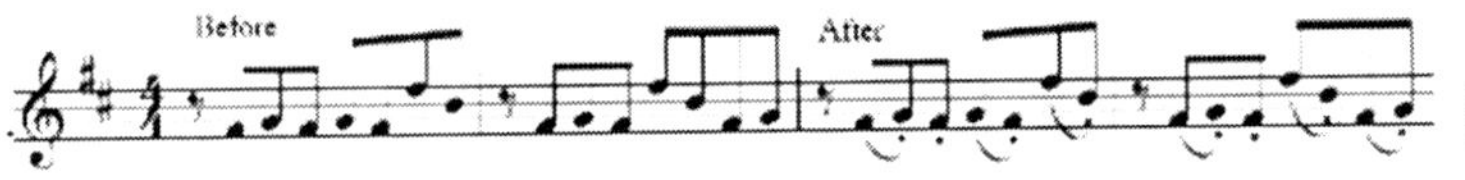

Example of before and after view of articulations

Before I began my research, I posed three key questions. Surprisingly, even though my curriculum was forced to change, it still addressed my three original questions: "How is performing in a small music group different from playing in a large band?" Many of the students felt greater pressure and concern with playing the music accurately, since there were fewer people responsible for each part. A positive benefit they noticed is that they were able to contribute more on a personal level to the direction of the music and gained a sense of ownership.

My second key question addressed the cultural relevance of the composer's life and history to the students. I was curious as to the effect, if any, on the student's interpretations of, or connection to, the music, if they found some aspect of Piazzolla's life or history relevant to their own lives. They were also happy to have had the chance to perform tango, because they had no previous exposure to its cultural roots. Moreover, knowledge of tango not only made it possible for them to play more stylistically, but to find a vivid place in their own worldview for this fresh music. In particular, with the roots of tango growing out of a bubble from the lower socio-economic classes, this meant a lot to students who by and large came from an economically and socially oppressed class.

My third question concerned the political atmosphere surrounding the interaction between popular and symphonic music. Piazzolla wrote a symphonic piece called *Sinfonia Buenos Aires* that enraged *tangueros (tango artists)* because they did not feel that an orchestra could play authentic tango. The orchestra players were also upset, because they did not think that popular music like tango belonged in the concert hall. Symphonic and popular music have always interacted, often at odds. But, whereas Haydn and Mozart effortlessly employed folk-inspired melodies in their symphonies, over the next century and a half a great divide evolved.

Based on my research, I came to the following conclusions for my key questions. All young musicians deserve an opportunity to experience small ensemble playing because it contributes to creativity, cooperative learning, higher musical awareness, leadership, and self-confidence. These attributes help them excel in life because they will be able to think creatively, problem solve, and be contributing members as part of a team.

Question	**% 4 or 5**
Through ArtsBridge I discovered my classmates' abilities.	55.6%
Through ArtsBridge I discovered my own abilities.	55.6%
Through ArtsBridge I had positive expression.	44.4%
Through ArtsBridge I became more interested in college.	55.6%
Through ArtsBridge I became more interested in a career in the arts.	66.7%
Through ArtsBridge I became more confident.	66.7%
Through ArtsBridge I became more involved in school.	44.4%
Through ArtsBridge I became more involved in the community.	33.3%
Through ArtsBridge I found school more enjoyable.	55.6%

The chart represents the percent of students who answered 4 or 5 on a scale of 1-5 with 1 representing the lowest value and 5 the highest.

When it came to cultural relevance, I realized that all students deserve to learn about the cultural and historical contributions of Latino & African-American composers. Many students do not get exposed to the contributions of great composers and musicians in the world of symphonic music outside of dead male European composers. Symphonic music has a much richer history than this Eurocentric paradigm. Having the opportunity to interact with the contributions of Latino and African-American composers will allow them more entry points into the diverse history of music.

In addition to my own observations of student progress, and their performance assessments, surveys were done to ascertain program impact on participants. Out of the 11 students, 9 were present for the evaluation day. The students were asked to rank their level of agreement with a set of questions on a scale of 1 (strongly disagree) to 5 (strongly agree). The results to the questions are shown in the chart above. Prior to working with the students, 66.7% of them planned on going to college and 33.3% were unsure. After the residency, 88.9% planned on going to college and 11.1% said they were still unsure.

Music has always evoked strong emotion and reactions. As early as the Renaissance, folk music has been incorporated in one form or another into instrumental, notated music. Today's folk music, closely related to popular music, has somehow lost its importance in many people's minds. Some modern music educators have decided to turn away from the rich contributions and culture of popular and world music, which unfortunately turns many students away from symphonic music or creates a disconnect between those who do perform. In order to keep young musicians involved in the music-making process, it is important that contemporary music educators continue to infuse their music programs with fresh, culturally relevant music. This can absolutely be done without sacrificing the quality and integrity of the music program. Young musicians should be encouraged to have the freedom to mix popular and symphonic music to create something new, just as Astor Piazzolla has done.

Notes

1   *A small, square accordion-like instrument popular in Latin America, especially for tango music*

2   *ArtsBridge is a national organization of universities in 13 states that confronts the dilemmas created by the elimination of the arts in many K-12 schools.*

3   *Gerri Mulligan (1927-1996) was an American jazz saxophonist, composer, and arranger. Johann Sebastian Bach (1685-1750) was a Baroque Composer. Giacomo Puccini (1858-1924) was a Romantic opera composer.*

BRINGING LITERATURE TO LIFE
THROUGH THEATER AND FILM

Iliana Phirippidis

The California education system is in dire need of repair—particularly the Los Angeles Unified School District (LAUSD). In his book, *City Schools and the American Dream: Reclaiming the Promise of Public Education*, Pedro Noguera points out that this is a national trend:

> *Urban school failure is pervasive. It is endemic in the nation's largest cities—New York, Chicago, Los Angeles, and Philadelphia, and not uncommon in small towns such as East St. Louis, Poughkeepsie, Camden, and Compton. In fact, wherever poor people are concentrated and employment is scarce, public schools are almost always very bad (Noguera 2003:3).*

The LAUSD is a prime example of this trend. In terms of standardized markers of proficiency, the numbers for LAUSD fall below 50% in all subject areas, which is an indicator that schools are not effectively teaching students. [1] Furthermore, a policy study on Arts Education in California conducted by Woodworth et. al. (2007) found that 72% of California's high schools fail to provide standards based Arts instruction in all four Arts disciplines, and that access to arts education is tied to socio-economic status. The statistics indicate that California schools are failing to provide students with a holistic education, or to prepare them to meet the "f" requirement in the Visual and Performing Arts for college admissions. Young people who study in schools in low socio-economic communities are disproportionately impacted by this failure.

While some may argue that arts are ancillary to a quality education, I contend that an integrated arts curriculum can enhance the quality of education and enrich students' understanding of traditional subjects. In this article, I discuss my experience with UCLA ArtsBridge—a program that emphasizes an integrated arts curriculum based on the Visual and Performing Arts Strands and the California Educational Standards in the Arts. Through this program, I taught integrated Theater and English in a 10th Grade Honors English class at David Starr Jordan High School (DSJHS) in Watts. According to the School Accountability Report Card for 2005-06, 9% of students at DSJHS reached proficient level or above in English and language arts, 2% in mathematics, 6% in science and 7% in history and social studies. By using the literature already assigned for the class as a basis for theater and film skills, I attempted to increase interest and enjoyment in learning, thus facilitating a richer and more complete learning environment. Basing my results mainly on student reflections and student artwork, I found that bringing Art into a classroom incorporates experiential learning (Dewey 1938) and a process of humanization in which students become producers of knowledge (Freire 1970). Students expressed a heightened interest in literature through drama and theater-related activities, understood the literature more, were able to better connect to the themes presented in class, and strengthened cooperative learning skills through collaborative project work.

Arts Education as Critical Pedagogy

There are many theorists who examine critical pedagogy, cultural studies, and their application to urban schooling, but Art is often left out of this dialogue as a marginal subject area.[2] It was apparent through my research that art greatly enhanced the learning process of the students with whom I had the honor of working, because it empowered students and validated their cultural capital. A more comprehensive theory for change in urban schools should include the arts as a core means for radical change. Although he does not directly address art, educational theorist Paolo Freire discusses the humanizing nature of liberatory pedagogy. In his book, *Pedagogy of the Oppressed,* Freire writes that:

> *Self-deprecation is [a] characteristic of the oppressed, which derives from their internalization of the opinion the oppressors hold of them. So often do they hear that they are good for nothing, know nothing and are incapable of learning anything…that in the end they become convinced of their own unfitness (Freire 1970:45).*

This describes the epidemic of students alienated from schools, giving up on themselves because they see that everyone else has as well. The dehumanizing nature of our current educational system blames students for failure on standardized tests, instead of examining the systems that fail students by not providing them the resources necessary to be successful in their education. Innovation and creativity in teaching is at stake because of the adoption of scripted literacy curricula like Open Court in the Los Angeles Unified School District.[3] With an increasing rigidity in course curriculum, schools are moving toward a conservative educational standard that ignores individual differences and relies on what Freire termed the "banking method" of education. Freire believed that "liberating education consists in acts of cognition, not transferals of information" (60). Art is just that—pure acts of cognition that draw from the personal experiences of students and turn students into creators and producers of knowledge.

Specifically, theater has been used as a pedagogical tool; a practice that is typified by the work of Augusto Boal's theater of the oppressed. Boal uses theater in a radical way, blurring the line between actor and spectator and creating activities that would challenge oppressive societal structures through art. His assertion in *Games for Actors and Non-*

Actors that "the theater is a weapon, and it is the people who should wield it," shows his impassioned belief in the power of theater to change society (Boal 1999: 122). Theater of the oppressed is an artistic method that requires critical thinking skills, while at the same time honoring the cultures and personal histories of its participants. When used in a critical way in a classroom, theater serves as a way for students to imagine possibilities within their lives and their communities. This was evident in improvisation games that we would play with the class in which students would come up with their own scene ideas. Scenes almost invariably involved situations from the lives of students or their friends -- this was the knowledge students brought with them into the classroom -- and theater was the mode by which they were able to think critically about those situations. The Arts can connect cognitive action to critical pedagogy, which, as can be seen by the following project analysis, is a deeply enriching tool for students' critical learning and development.

The Project

Fellow ArtsBridge scholar Jena McRae and I were paired with a then third year English and Theater teacher at DSJHS — Kori Hamilton. Hamilton was enthusiastic to have McRae and me as arts teachers once a week in both her Advanced Acting and her 10th Grade Honors English classes. Once the planning stages began, we decided that I would lead the English class, and McRae, coming from a stronger theater background, would be in charge of the Advanced Acting class. When planning my curriculum, I first decided on the basic theater skill set I wanted my students to have at the end of the residency. This included improvisation skills, scriptwriting, character analysis, performance techniques, set design, and basic video operation. I also studied the reading list Hamilton had already planned out for her course so that I could find ways to integrate these skills into her curriculum. My goals were to use theater and film to bring literature to life and enrich student understanding while increasing participation in the classroom.

Planning for the residency involved three observation days in Hamilton's classroom and multiple development meetings in which the three of us gathered to discuss curriculum, scheduling, and goals. During the course of my residency, the students and I read *Something Wicked This Way Comes* by Ray Bradbury, *Like Water for Chocolate* by Laura Esquivel, and *Macbeth* by William Shakespeare. With both the literature and skill set goals in mind, I was able to create a curriculum to enhance the overall class. The residency consisted of 16 sessions, each 90 minutes long. In the first session, an introduction to improvisation in theater, there was an overall sense of shyness from the students. It may have been that they were still uneasy about new teachers in the classroom, or it may have been that they lacked the experience of being up in front of their classmates. By the middle of our residency, the students were more comfortable presenting their work in front of the class. Building confidence helped several students overcome their shyness. Dalia, for example, was incredibly shy and even wrote in one of her journal reflections that "getting up in front of the class was my least favorite part because I was really shy, but now it's not so hard."

Something Wicked This Way Comes

We began the second session with work from the first novel. The students seemed alienated by *Something Wicked This Way Comes*, complaining that it was boring. They didn't understand the story and thought it was a strange book. Using as much descriptive writing as possible, I gave them an activity that would help them with character analysis. I assigned the students different characters, and they worked in groups or pairs to describe them. We then set up scenes from various chapters of the book so that each student was playing the character he or she had just worked on developing.

The third session comprised a scriptwriting workshop in which we brainstormed about what should be included in a script and its various components. The students seemed to know all of the parts that made up a script, such as setting, characters, stage direction and dialogue, so I passed out worksheets for a partner activity. The worksheets had dialogues from *Something Wicked This Way Comes,* and the students were asked to identify the objectives of each of the characters, add a setting and stage direction, and write a dialogue. After we discussed the handouts, the students acted out their scenes. The creativity of the students in how they decided to complete their dialogues was inspiring, because it showed how engaged they were with the material. Additionally, providing a space for creativity gave students agency in a piece of literature that was previously inaccessible to them. Now the students were able to visualize the scenes from the novel and alternative plots, which helped them to think critically about the text. The last project for *Something Wicked This Way Comes* was a set design project in which students were asked to find quotes from the novel describing a particular setting, then to visually represent that setting as if it were the set of a play. This activity gave those shyer students a chance to truly shine and to express themselves visually in a normally literature-based classroom.

Like Water for Chocolate

In trying to find a way to link theater skills with the novel *Like Water for Chocolate*, and along with Hamilton's chosen topic of cultural identity, I came across an activity described by Frank McCourt in his autobiography, *Teacher Man*. The activity involved the dramatic readings of recipes out of a cookbook. I decided that this would be a fun and interesting way to explore students' perceptions of cultural identity and how they envisioned their own identity in relation to their culture. I asked students to bring in a recipe from home - something they love to eat, something their family cooks, something they like to cook - any type of recipe they wanted. The students were slightly confused by my request, not knowing what I was going to ask them to do with these recipes, but they brought them in anyway. We then turned these recipes into creative monologues; students decided on a character or a style of reading and presented it to the class. The performances included a torta recipe where the student acted as a chef at King Taco Restaurant, a recipe for "Daddy's Famous French Fries," and even "Nubia's Cooking Show." This activity was not only fun and entertaining, but it gave students another way to connect to the literature as well as to bring an aspect of their own culture into the classroom.

Macbeth

Finally, knowing that the students would be reading Shakespeare's *Macbeth*, I wanted to create a project that would draw upon all of the skills we had developed before, as well as to introduce filmmaking and to give the students the opportunity to create a lasting piece of art. The project was Macbeth MiniMovies, a collaborative group video project based on a scene from Macbeth. I split the class up into four small cooperative learning groups and asked them to decide who from their group would take the position of director, videographer, set designers, and actors. I then assigned them a scene from *Macbeth* and asked them to rewrite the scene using a specific modern setting, or changing the context in some way to make it appeal to a modern audience. The students rewrote the scripts, created sets and found costumes, learned how to use video cameras to record and edit, and put together films—all in 3 days. Their creativity and diligence were amazing, and although this was clearly a challenge for them, they seemed to thoroughly enjoy it at the same time. This was the first time many of the students had been introduced to film, so the excitement of working with a new genre was apparent.

Engaged Learning

Even though the class I worked with was an Honors English class, there were still a number of students who were under-prepared or who chose not to attend class. In the recent CST standardized test, this class had a 90% passing rate on the English section, although only 9 out of 25 students passed at "proficient" or "advanced" level. This is not the fault of the students or the teacher, rather a culmination of years of inadequate schooling. The result is a disengagement that can begin to be countered by the introduction of arts into the curriculum. Arts are not only a creative outlet, but they are also a means for Dewey's experiential learning. Dewey contends that:

As an individual passes from one situation to another, his world, his environment, expands or contracts. He does not find himself living in another world but in a different part or aspect of one and the same world. What he has learned in the way of knowledge and skill in one situation becomes an instrument of understanding and dealing effectively with the situations which follow (Dewey 1938:44).

A revolutionary form of education, then, must draw on the experiences of the students; art is one way to do this. Even when students were completing dialogues for a scriptwriting workshop for *Something Wicked This Way Comes*, they came up with ideas about how the characters would respond to a given situation based on their own personal experiences. Taking the activity a step further and having students act out the scenes put themselves in the position of the characters and become actively engaged in the literature. The recipe monologue activity also engaged students by drawing on lived experience and by honoring a part of the students' personal history in the classroom. By asking students to bring material for our class that they identified with culturally, I attempted to shift the perceptions of who is a teacher and who is a student within the classroom. The recipe monologues became opportunities for the students to teach the rest of us about a particular food item from their lives. Most students performed the monologues as a type of cooking lesson—whether it was an older sibling or grandmother teaching a young child how to cook, or a chef at a restaurant teaching a new worker a certain recipe. Beyond the mere performance aspect, students really became teachers and were engaged in theater skills and in understanding how they could connect personally to the stories within *Like Water for Chocolate*, a novel that starts each chapter with a recipe. There was a conscious effort to move away from what Paolo Freire calls the "banking" education because "The capability of banking education to minimize or annul the students' creative power and to stimulate their credulity serves the interests of the oppressors" (Freire 1970:54). Banking education assumes that the teacher is the bearer of all knowledge and the students are a blank slate to be filled by information—it is unidirectional and does not account for knowledge already held by the students. This is the perception of the teacher-student relationship that the students' monologues challenged. Art requires the knowledge and experience that students already possess, and it validates this knowledge as important. Therefore, when students are presented with activities in which their culture and knowledge is valued and in which they enjoy the learning process, they become much more engaged in the core curriculum as well.

Enriched Understanding

The clearest indicators that students gained an enriched understanding of literature and literary themes is from the reflections of the students themselves. Students kept journals throughout the ArtsBridge residency and also wrote a final reflection about their experience with the program. Reyna, a student who seemed disengaged from classroom activities at the beginning of the residency, wrote: "What helped me understand the book was when people went up and acted out the scenes and [when we] did scriptwriting. I really liked set design, because it helped me visualize the scenery and the book better." She had initially been hesitant to participate in acting activities due to her shyness, but when she was given the opportunity to do visual art, her talents shone brightly. Even when she was nervous to perform, the activities as a whole helped her understand the literature in a more meaningful way than she had previously. Every student alluded to the acting and set design activities as the parts of the residency that helped them understand the literature better; therefore every student felt that their learning had been enhanced through the Arts. Furthermore, they articulated their ability to help peers understand literature better through the Macbeth MiniMovie Film activity. Jesus, Konyko, and Joana expressed in their interview that they thought their MiniMovie should be seen by all students reading *Macbeth* because, it helped them better understand the play. Jesus noted, "Students might not understand Shakespeare's language, but if they see our film then maybe they can understand the play better." The level of understanding moved beyond a consumption of knowledge. Students became producers of knowledge through the filmmaking process and saw their films as pedagogical tools. This is a profound example of the rejection of the banking method of education; this is students taking control of the learning process with the teacher as the facilitator. The MiniMovie project was almost entirely student-run, and the results were creative, effective, and brought more joy and excitement into the classroom, deeply enriching student learning.

Collaboration and Honoring Multiple Literacies

Although every project in the residency involved group or partner work, the Macbeth MiniMovie project exemplified student collaboration and teamwork, building critical problem solving skills as well as highlighting individual talents of each student. The four cooperative learning groups were asked to decide amongst themselves who would be the director, the videographer, the set designer, and the actors; the selection process was organically democratic. Students with leadership tendencies stood up as directors; the visual artists became set designers; technologically inclined students became videographers; and those who enjoyed acting became the actors. Some students filled multiple roles. The groups came across many obstacles in the course of the project, beginning with understanding the scene that had been assigned to them and creating their own version of the script. Once this hurdle had been jumped, production work began, and a true process of collaboration could be seen. In one group, which decided to turn their scene into a pirate theme, the set designers used black garbage bags to cover a part of the outside of the classroom, and they made a pirate flag and plank as part of their ship. While they built the set, the actors worked on their lines and the director and videographer made a storyboard of their MiniMovie to ensure that the shoot could be done in a short amount of time. The success of their project was dependent upon their ability to bring individual skills to the table, to communicate readily, and to compromise and adapt to changing situations. Shaqueal, an actress in the Pirates group, noted the challenge of working with a group, admitting, "It was hard working together with other students I didn't know that well, but we did it and now I know them a lot better." She and other students felt that bonds with their classmates had been made through this teamwork process.

Working in collaborative groups also gave students the opportunity to share their own talents or to develop new ones. The introduction of alternative types of literacy within an English class that encouraged advanced critical thinking meant that students were using their talents in an effective way. One student who did not pass her last standardized test was the main actress in her group's MiniMovie, for which she also helped write the script. She had approached me one day in class as she was depressed about her test score and lacking confidence in her own capabilities as an English student. At the end of the project, she had a firm understanding of *Macbeth*, could articulate the challenges and triumphs of working with her group, and was proud of her acting and of their final film. All too often standardized testing and the standardization of curriculum can have detrimental effects on the self-confidence of students. Bringing Art into the English classroom showed students the importance of their multiple literacies and how these can be used to help with the traditional ones. Essentially, both traditional and non-traditional literacies are needed for a well-rounded education.

Implications for the Future

The personal implications of my involvement in the ArtsBridge project are two-fold. First, learning how to integrate multiple literacies in the Arts into a core standardized curriculum will influence my own curriculum development as a teacher in the future. Second, seeing how art has the ability to foster critical pedagogy in an urban classroom will influence my goal to advocate for arts education on a policy level. This program was my first endeavor teaching in a classroom, standing before a class of students and offering my knowledge and direction toward a common goal of learning. At times it was stressful, exciting, and, ultimately, my most rewarding experience as a student at UCLA. Other times it was the only time I felt engaged in the city beyond the campus walls. This aspect of service learning is vital to the undergraduate experience, especially in the education and arts disciplines, because it is a tangible experience and the effects are visible. The only way to understand urban education is to work within it, and the only way to understand how Arts can be involved in education is to see it in action. I cannot imagine feeling prepared to advance to post-graduate school or enter the workforce without this practical teaching experience; furthermore, the program's emphasis on critical pedagogy in the classroom was a fitting culmination to my prior involvement in the education minor, which also uses critical pedagogy as a core theory.

The institutional implications for ArtsBridge are always under scrutiny. Budget cutbacks consistently threaten to restructure or eliminate the program altogether, which would be a devastating blow for the progressive education movement at UCLA. While there are many outreach and service learning programs, few stress the necessity of quality Arts education in urban schools. It is clear from my personal research and the research of fellow ArtsBridge scholars that the concept of integrated arts curriculum is working. One scholar in my group cohort, Amy Chou, developed an "Art of Scientific Observation" residency, fusing visual art and science. Another scholar, Cynthia Wennstrom, had great results teaching visual art in a supported reading and writing middle school English course. Yet another scholar in our group, Desiree Gallardo, taught a course on Polynesian dance that stressed self-confidence and positive self-image for young women in a high school physical education class. These are just a few examples of the types of creative projects developed by enthusiastic and talented undergraduate and graduate ArtsBridge scholars, who will some day make greater changes in the education field. Critical pedagogy and the Arts is an exciting new concept that is still undergoing many changes; however, the successes of programs like ArtsBridge is undeniable. The future of critical urban education depends on the synergy of a quality arts program alongside a humanizing core curriculum.

Notes

1   Paolo Freire, Jurgen Habermas, Ivan Illich, Antonio Gramsci, Peter McLaren, Douglas Kellner

2   Open Court is a systematic reading and phonics program developed by SRA-McGraw Hill used in many public elementary schools.

3   https://www.sraonline.com/oc_home.html

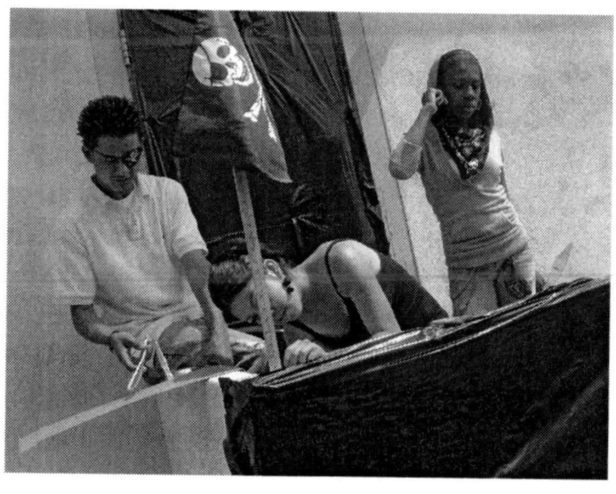

STORYTELLING, DANCE, AND HUMAN ANATOMY

Lindsay Lindberg

Becoming a teaching artist through the ArtsBridge program has been a life changing experience, as I was given the opportunity to explore my dancing through new venues and points of views as teacher and performer. Integrating anatomy into the dance studio at Gabriella Charter School (GCS) was an idea that I had pondered for several months, so I was ecstatic to have the opportunity to teach second graders. Since GCS students already have an hour of dancing built into their regular school curriculum, the basic dance class I had initially envisioned was no longer appropriate. I eventually decided to design a curriculum based on dance and human anatomy that coincided with my potential interest in pursuing a career in physical therapy through the UCLA Sports Medicine Internship Program. I chose to focus my project on the anatomical aspects of the human body for my own benefit as much as for the tremendous learning opportunity it presented for my students. I used a model skeleton, that I playfully called Mr. Bones, as a useful visual aid for the children. To help make the material more accessible, I also used classic stories to engage them with the curriculum.

Over a four-month period, I taught the same group of 20 second grade students each week for a 45 minute lesson. These brief sessions were both a challenge and a rewarding experience. The students' small size and attention spans proved beneficial as they were eager to learn. Teaching a new anatomical concept while simultaneously integrating it into a dance class was my main challenge as there never seemed to be enough time in each session.

One day, while deeply enthralled by the teaching experience at Gabriella Charter School and surrounded by the stunning murals painted by the parent volunteers, I heard myself trying to explain the function of the scapula bones in terms that would be memorable to a second grader. I instantly remembered the Greek myth of Iccarus and his father, Daedalus. This quasi-tragic tale, which I adapted to make more appropriate and understandable, is riveting for second graders as it takes them on a journey to a place far removed from the dance studio, harnessing their imagination, and releasing their creativity into the lesson. The tale tells of a father and son who are trapped in an island tower, when the only hope of escape entails flying over miles of ocean back to the mainland. Carefully, they build two sets of wings out of molten candle wax and painstakingly collected bird feathers; one set for each of them. On the day they finally embark on their journey, the son flies too close to the sun against his father's warnings, the wings are incinerated, and the young man falls to his death in the churning ocean. The pedagogical effect of the story had re-shaped the way I approached teaching Dance and Human Anatomy to young children.

Initially, the incorporation of storytelling seemed like the easiest thing to do.

The students loved the story, and it deeply influenced their physical embodiment of the scapula, helping them accurately envision the inner workings of their body. But gradually it became clear to me that my once fully focused dance class had become overwhelmed by the terms and anatomical coloring worksheets. To get back on track I realized that I had to shorten the stories so as to have more time for dance. The ArtsBridge program has helped me better understand the potency and overpowering effects the spoken word can have in a classroom. Coupling my words with the enabling power of movement has been an interesting experience. To my surprise, with an appropriate proportion of movement to verbal communication, the multifaceted aspects of dance and human anatomy can be easily taught, shared, and expressed.

The human body is a glorious piece of art we can each use advantageously. Occasionally, we may all take it for granted, but it is important for each individual to have at least a conceptual understanding of how our magnificent machines enable and surreptitiously shape every course of action we take. In order to introduce this concept to a studio filled with young, eager, shining faces, I broke my residency down into three basic units; the skeletal, muscular, and circulatory systems.

The skeletal system is the unit we began with first, in which we covered the axial skeleton, scapula, humorous, patella, and hip bones, with a weekly performance by Mr. Bones, the skeleton. The primary story permeating the skeletal unit was of Iccarus and Daedalus. The story informed our movements, physical explorations, and class discussions while incorporating multiple visual and performing arts standards (VAPA). Musculature was next in our whirlwind second grade style tour of the body. Here we studied the two primary calf muscles, the soleus and gastrocnemius, and the famed Achilles tendon. Not surprisingly, the story to tie these anatomical building blocks together was the Greek myth of Achilles, the great warrior. [1] The third and final unit was the circulatory system, which was by far the biggest conceptual challenge for the students to grasp. The idea of the blood stream was difficult to grapple with, and even more difficult to physically embody. Here I utilized red and white silk squares of fabric to visually represent red blood cells that deliver oxygen and white blood cells that fight infection. [2] The class enacted VAPA standard 2.6 "Create, memorize, and perform original expressive movements for peers" without excluding standards 1.4, 4.2, 5.1 or 5.4 sacrificing any knowledge intake.

The key questions that drove my curriculum were as follows. First, how does incorporating anatomy into dance impact student learning? Second, how can storytelling support dance learning? And finally, can including anatomy in the dance education process help to prevent future injuries? The student responses I received were most insightful and showed me that my students were retaining the information and benefiting from my classes. One second grader remarked that, "It is fun to dance because you get to flex your body and get a lot of energy" (Belay, 30 May 2008). She was immediately followed by Kevin Diaz, who shared his opinion by explaining to me that "People might get interested in [dance] because it's something that people like a lot and you get to move your body" (Diaz, 30 May 2008).

I found the storytelling component the most interesting aspect of teaching dance as it became a core instructional component. Out of curiosity I asked my students what which were their favorite stories and why. Each child had his or her own reasons for picking a favorite story; some preferred the story of "Theseus," half bull and half man (commonly known to those over the age of seven as Iccarus) and "the little frog," the tale of Jeremy Fisher (Ramirez and Kim, 30 May 2008).[3] One of the most vibrant dance memories I was able to record was a recitation of the class exercises we practiced after learning about our hinging knee joints and hips and hearing the story of the fishing frog. "There was one line that was the fish, and then the other line was the frog….We got to do the knees, and we got to do the fish because we had to jump" with our knees (Gutierrez, 30 May 2008). Their answers were all the validation I needed to confirm that the storytelling time had not been a waste. The students took many valuable lessons from the stories, and they now have a multi-dimensional view of the human body and of dance.

The most rewarding question I asked my students was simple and straightforward: "What has Mr. Bones helped you learn about your body?" My students astounded me in reciting verbatim not only the multiple stories I had shared with them, but the specific anatomical terms we had covered months ago. Even the smallest things I may have mentioned as a cast-off comment were what some of my students remembered the most vividly from the entire residency, small catch phrases they used to their own advantage to remember the new vocabulary.

By integrating components of human anatomy into each dance lesson, I introduced the students to new ways of noticing and controlling their movements, expressing themselves clearly, and guided them to understand that they are in control of their bodies as well as their futures. Integrating storytelling, anatomy, and dance allows young learners to better discover the magic of their own bodies. Stories and skeletons can help children imagine what their bodies are made of and how they work, and incorporating anatomy into dance education sets the ground work for future injury prevention and body awareness. Dance can influence every choice one makes throughout a lifetime; and by integrating anatomy into the dance studio, I was able to underscore the importance and achievability of a healthy, creative lifestyle.

Interviews

Belay, Ruth. 2008. Personal interview with the author, May 30.
Diaz, Kevin. 2008. Personal interview with the author, May 30.
Guitierrez, Melanii. 2008. Personal interview with the author, May 30.
Kim, Roy. 2008. Personal interview with the author, May 30.
Ramirez, Emanuel. 2008. Personal interview with the author, May 27.

Notes

1   *The VAPA standards played with here were again 1.4, 4.2. This unit also introduced standard 5.1 to "use literature to inspire dance ideas" and 5.4 where we "describe[d] how dancing requires good health-related habits."*

2   *The class enacted VAPA standard 2.6 to "create, memorize, and perform original expressive movements for peers" without excluding standards 1.4, 4.2, 5.1 or 5.4 sacrificing any knowledge intake.*

3   *In this tale a frog goes fishing for his dinner, and is, in the end, defeated by the fish he intended to catch.*

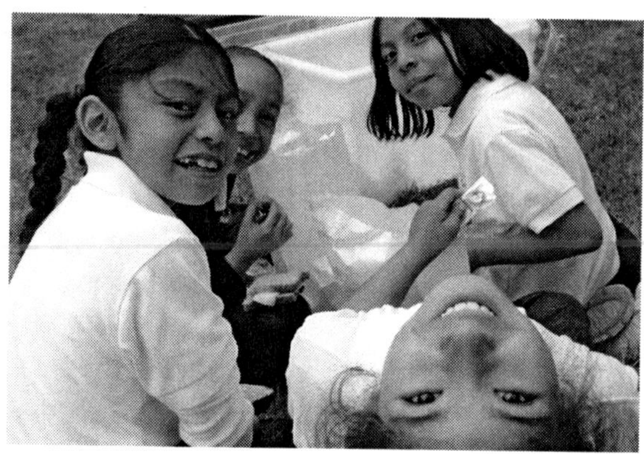

DANCING FOR HEALTH[1]

Norlyn Asprec

Introduction

Childhood obesity has become a growing public health issue in the United States and is considered to be the most threatening disease in the country. Recently, First Lady Michelle Obama acknowledged the gravity of the problem by establishing the national *Let's Move* campaign to combat childhood obesity. There is controversy about characterizing obesity either as a disease or a serious health concern. I choose to refer to obesity as a disease, because it significantly impairs health and proper body functioning. There are several health risks and conditions associated with obesity, such as Type II diabetes, stroke, hypertension, and some cancers. The most recent estimates attribute 3.2 percent of all new cancers - 14 percent of cancer deaths in men and 20 percent in women - to obesity (National Cancer Institute 2008). Obesity also has economic consequences since the costs of obesity treatments affect United States healthcare spending. In 2004, the estimated health care costs related to overweight and obese categories range from $98 billion to $129 billion (Partnership for Prevention 2008). Childhood obesity can be prevented, but unfortunately there has been a lack of coordinated interventions. In order to develop effective solutions, partnerships between the federal, state, and local governments and community need to be created. This article expands on the strengths of community action and dance education for health in confronting childhood obesity in urban communities.

Defining Childhood Obesity

Childhood obesity is a health problem that affects all children across the country due to the lack of nutritious foods in school lunches, fast food restaurants and junk food. The terms "obesity" or "overweight" are defined by the Center for Disease Control (CDC) as a body mass index (BMI) at or above the 95th percentile for children of the same age and sex (Center for Disease Control 2008). Body Mass Index is a number calculated from the child's weight and height, and it is a reliable calculation for the amount of body fat for children. This definition is based on the 2000 CDC growth charts for the United States.

In figure 1, data is shown from two National Health and Nutrition Examination Surveys (NHANES) which were conducted in 1976–1980 and 2003–2004. The table shows there has been a significant growth of overweight youth from the 1960s through 2004. For children ages 2–5 years, prevalence increased from 5 percent to 13.9 percent, for those ages 6–11 years, from 6.5 percent to 18.8 percent, and for those ages 12–19 years, from 5.0 percent to 17.4 percent (National Center for Health Statistics 2008). The factors that attributed to the high increase of overweight youth included less physical activity, increased consumption in foods high in fat, increased hours of watching television and playing video games.

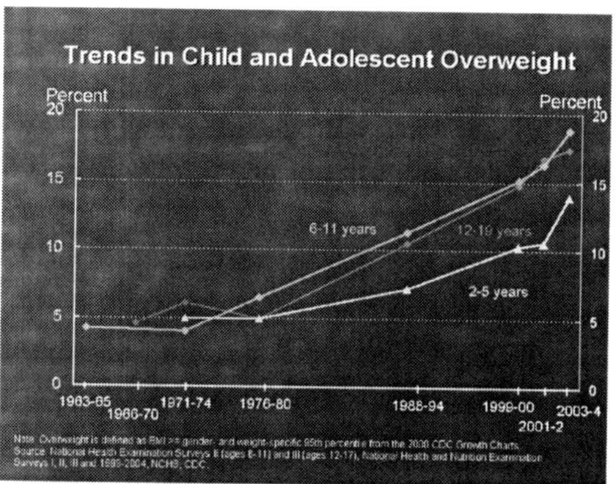

*Fig 1. National Health and Nutrition Examination
Surveys I, II, III and 1999-2004, NCHC, CDC*

Childhood obesity also disproportionately affects children from low-income families in comparison to children of higher income (Kumanyika 2006:188). The Surgeon General states, "Overweight and obesity are particularly common among minority groups and those with a lower family income" (U.S. Department of Health and Human Services 2001). Some of the reasons for this include inadequate access to fresh fruits and vegetables, safe streets, and recreational facilities. These resources are the necessary tools needed to encourage children to live an active and healthy lifestyle. In a research study, obesity rates were as high as 30% in the lowest income neighborhoods, compared to about 5% in the most affluent zip codes (Drewnowski 2007). It is important to understand the demographics of the Los Angeles area in relation to the obesity epidemic. According to the United States Census Bureau, the estimated population of the Los Angeles Unified School District is 4,612,289, constituting 194,010 children 5 to 17 years old who are in poverty (U.S. Census Bureau 2008).

Community Actions and Public Policy

Childhood obesity is a significant public health issue that raises questions concerning social justice. In order to reduce health disparities in communities, it is important that the urban environment supports health and promotes physical activity. People who are of low socio-economic status and who live in urban environments deserve the right to have access to fresh fruits and vegetables. They also deserve to have safe streets like those in communities of higher socio-economic status.

In order to understand how public policy and community action interact, I took a top down and bottom up approach. I was a nutrition and dance teacher for the ArtsBridge program in South Los Angeles, and I also interned for the California Healthcare Institute in Washington D.C. with the UCLA Center for American Politics and Public Policy. These two experiences aided my understanding of childhood obesity in urban Los Angeles and allowed me to use the skills I developed in the classroom and apply them to the community and vice versa. As an ArtsBridge scholar, I took part in local community building activities and saw how neighborhood efforts can address local needs. My internship in Washington D.C. expanded my knowledge of health policy as I attended health briefings around the capitol and was introduced to various health issues and possible health solutions. I also learned from various health organizations that the new administration should focus on chronic disease prevention in addition to healthcare coverage.

In response to the political nature of this health issue, all three levels of government: local, state, and federal have proposed possible solutions to improve the health of youth. For example, in my work in South Los Angeles, local community organizations, such as Strategic Economic Enterprises Los Angeles (SEE-LA), have intervened and established farmer's markets to make fresh produce more accessible. At the state level, the government has developed and established policies to improve the nutritional value of school meals and drinks. Further, policy makers at the federal level have been asking Congress to invest in preventing chronic disease. On February 16, 2007 a legislative House bill, H.R.1163 titled "Stop Obesity in Schools Act 2007," was introduced to Congress (Library of Congress, Thomas 2009). However, Congress has not taken the step to focus on preventive health, and the bill was referred to the Subcommittee on Health. Childhood obesity legislation is being introduced to Congress, and federal action is needed to address and prevent this health problem.

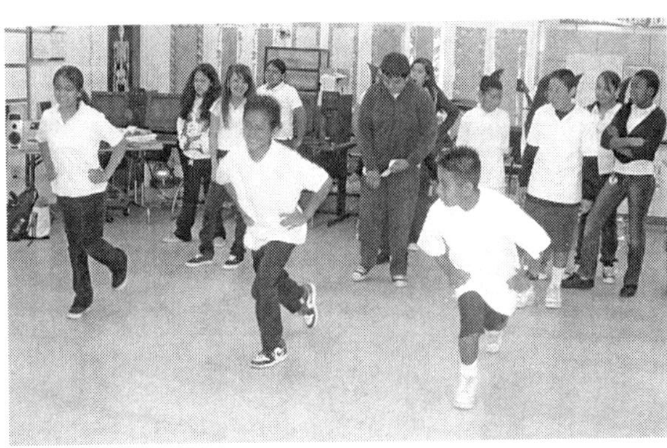

Fig 2. Students study dancing for health at Carver Middle School

Dance and Health Education Through ArtsBridge

As a UCLA undergraduate, I participated in the ArtsInitiative (ArtsIn) Scholar Program with the UCLA Academic Advancement Program and identified my research interest in dance and childhood obesity prevention. When I started teaching dance and nutrition classes to sixth grade students, many of them were unfamiliar with dance expression and movement in class. The goal of my curriculum was to encourage the students to be physically active and to become more aware of their daily food choices. I also wanted the students to use dance as a form of creative expression. I developed a dance and health curriculum emphasizing ballet and jazz. I decided to start with ballet, because I consider it to be the foundation to developing strong jazz dance technique. However, the students were not responsive to the ballet portion of my curriculum. They participated in class, but they did not welcome or show enthusiasm. As a result, I tailored my dance curriculum to the students' interests and decided to teach them contemporary choreography. I choreographed a dance using jazz and hip-hop movements to the song *"Superstar"* by Lupe Fiasco. There was noticeably more energy and focus from the students than when I had started teaching jazz and hip-hop technique. I gained 100% participation from the students. I also recognized the importance of cultural relevancy in dance programs because it affirms the identity of the youth.

On the other hand, I struggled with a lack of access to dance space and teaching a dance curriculum in the track system. While the multiple track system is aimed to be phased out in the future, GWCMS is one of the last Los Angeles Unified School District middle schools still in that system due to overcrowding. Having access to dance space is necessary to have an effective movement class because students need a place to move and perform the choreography. There was a physical education classroom, but I was not granted access to that space, and, therefore, resorted to teaching my class in a small classroom. It was also a challenge teaching the students on a track system which with its lack of consistency in sequential learning hinders student progress. After the students came back from a one to two month break, I had to begin again teaching the students basic dance technique instead of progressing with more challenging movement. The track system made it difficult for the students to retain information and made it difficult for me to reach my student learning objectives.

Nevertheless, Arts integration has the potential to contribute to student learning (Rabkin 2004:149). Arts education programs such as ArtsBridge have a significant impact on students and their peers. According to the ArtsBridge end of the year evaluation (2008), data collected assessed program impact on the issues related to self-awareness, self-esteem, and positive peer relationships (Shimshon-Santo 2008:4). Over half of the students (55.4%) reported that they discovered new talents or abilities in themselves as a result of program participation, and 49.5% of the participants reported that they discovered new talents or abilities in their classmates (Shimshon-Santo 2008:4). The program also affected student expression. After participation, 53.4% of the students felt more able to express themselves in positive ways.

Unfortunately, establishing Arts integrated curriculum in schools is difficult because the American education system faces other challenges, such as budget cuts and uninformed district policy decisions. In order to establish a successful arts integrated program, educators and education policymakers must embrace arts integration as an effective and practical strategy for improving schools and student performance at all levels (Rabkin 2004:145).

Local Nutrition

George Washington Carver Middle School engages in local efforts by allowing SEE-LA to offer a farmer's market on Saturdays in the staff parking lot and opens its field space to neighborhood youth soccer leagues on the weekends. During the five months I taught dance and nutrition classes as an ArtsBridge Scholar at GWCMS, I met with Pompea Smith, CEO of SEE-LA and their cooking instructor, Laura Gonzales. In addition, faculty members of GWCMS joined us - Thomas Turner, Leonard Choi and my guiding teacher, Sonja Williams. During our meetings at the farmer's market we discussed the current health needs of the students and their families and how SEE-LA's cooking classes and farmer's markets might complement my nutrition and dance curriculum for the sixth grade GWCMS students. The cooking classes would be beneficial to the students and their parents, because they could inform them of the importance of nutrition as well as teach the families how to cook nutritious, cultural dishes that are low in fat.

The challenge to the farmer's market at GWCMS was low participation, due to the limited ability of residents to use Women, Infant, Children (WIC) or food stamps to purchase fresh fruits and vegetables. SEE-LA subsidizes food prices at the location to bring down costs and also accepts food stamps and WIC. However, the number of fresh food coupons that could be used was far less than sufficient to keep fresh foods and vegetables on the tables of local households year round.

In addition to attending local community meetings, I also observed GWCMS's cafeteria. I wanted to see what foods the students were given at lunch and if fresh fruits and vegetables were made available. When I visited, the students had a choice of salads, rice bowls, and chicken wings as well as bananas and oranges for lunch. I observed that most of the students would take the fruit from the cafeteria, but would either throw it away or leave it on the school bench. The students could purchase snacks at break time, including cookies, cheese balls and pretzels. Non-carbonated drinks such as Gatorade, apple juice, orange juice and lemonade were also available. The school did not permit students to have carbonated drinks, chips, or candy bars.

The types of foods and drinks made available to students of the Los Angeles Unified School District are a result of the soda and junk food ban. "The Los Angeles Unified School District passed a soda vending ban that went into effect in January 2004.

A further ban on fried chips, candy, and other snack foods in school vending machines and stores went into effect in July 2004" (Story 2006:123). The soda and junk food ban in Los Angeles was a positive effort to improve student health, but limiting junk food is not enough. My Guiding Teacher, Sonja Williams, explained that most students buy junk food from a store near the school. Therefore, it is important to see local food choices as a local rather than school wide issue. At school, students need to be encouraged to eat fruits and vegetables, and health teachers need to facilitate the students' understanding of nutrition and health. This would require a broad-based local health education campaign informing both children and adults.

The local government in the South Los Angeles area has attempted to broaden nutrition policy beyond school campuses. In 2008, Jan Perry, Councilwoman of the 9th District, which includes most of the South Los Angeles area, introduced a measure to ban new fast-food restaurants in South Los Angeles for a year (Hennessy 2008:1). The County Department of Public Health released a study showing that 30% of South Los Angeles adults were obese, compared with about 21% of adults countywide. South L.A. also has the highest incidence of diabetes in the county, 11.7% compared with 8.1% for the county as a whole (1). While there are about 8,200 restaurants in the area higher than in the Westside, downtown, or Hollywood, South Los Angeles also has fewer grocery stores. Finding that obesity and diabetes are both prevalent in her district, Perry proposed the ban as an attempt to better the health of the residents in the area.

Another barrier to living healthy is the lack of safe streets in the neighborhood. GWCMS itself is a safe environment for children and adults. However, like most Los Angeles urban neighborhoods, gang violence is a real threat to local residents. During my residency, there was a gang related shooting at a bus stop near GWCMS and the children rushed back into the school site for shelter. I also found out from my class that most of them get a ride to school rather than walk due to the safety issue. An unsafe environment can hinder physical activity and prevent a healthy lifestyle.

A study conducted by the Center for Disease Control surveyed households with children between the ages of five and eighteen about the reasons why their children don't walk or bike to school. The study found the reasons to be long distances, traffic danger, crime, bad weather, and school policy (Martin 2005). Rather than blame schools for local violence, inner city schools need to be supported properly to continue to provide a refuge for local youth. However, it takes policy initiatives, community activists, teachers, non-profit organizations, and community partners like ArtsBridge to find tangible solutions to bring policy imperatives to life at the local level.

Recommendations

Helpful policy options for schools include providing regular creative options for physical education, which has been reduced dramatically over the last decade because of competing education requirements and funding constraints. Faculty and administrators at school campuses need to become invested in public health. Physical education teachers can engage students in class through creative activities and encourage students to be physically active outside of school, but physical education classes are regularly overcrowded and undervalued.

My own analysis is supported by the findings in *The Health Care Delivery System: A Blueprint for Reform* (2008), which argues that public policy can help reduce obesity and physical inactivity in the United States. The Center for American Progress recommends that the U.S. Department of Agriculture update nutritional standards for school lunches and the President expand the department's authority over alternative foods, such as items sold in vending machines, during or after school, since unhealthy food choices outside the schools are sometimes in competition with the healthier school lunch program (Center for American Progress 2008:105). The blueprint also recommends the importance of grants to provide access to fresh produce in low-income areas. It states, "Obesity prevention initiatives targeting diet generally attempt to increase access to healthy foods and increase transparency of nutritional content. The federal government should expand these initiatives by providing grants through the Department of Agriculture by encouraging entry of new grocery stores, farmers markets, and cooperatives into underserved neighborhoods" (Center for American Progress 2008:105).

In conclusion, it is essential that approaches to childhood obesity prevention consider location, socio-economic status, and culture. Residents who live in urban neighborhoods are at an increased risk for obesity due to the lack of access to grocery stores with fresh produce and safe streets. Obesity can result in serious chronic diseases such as diabetes, stroke, and heart disease. Safe places for physical activity and access to healthy food choices in the community support obesity prevention. Dance education is beneficial as a physical education alternative that affirms youth identity and culture. Therefore, health education can benefit from arts education, and when linked to disease prevention, policy and community action, can improve children's health.

Notes

1   *All health information not otherwise referenced was retrieved from the following organizations and their websites:*

Center for American Progress and the Institute of Medicine. www.americanprogress.org

National Center for Health Statistics, Center for Disease Control. www.cdc.gov/nchs

National Cancer Institute. www.cancer.gov

National Center for Health Statistics. www.cancer.gov/ncicancerbulletin

The Library of Congress, Thomas. "Bills, Resolutions." http://thomas.loc.gov

U. S. Census Bureau. www.censusbureau.gov

U.S. Department of Health and Human Services. www.censusbureau.gov

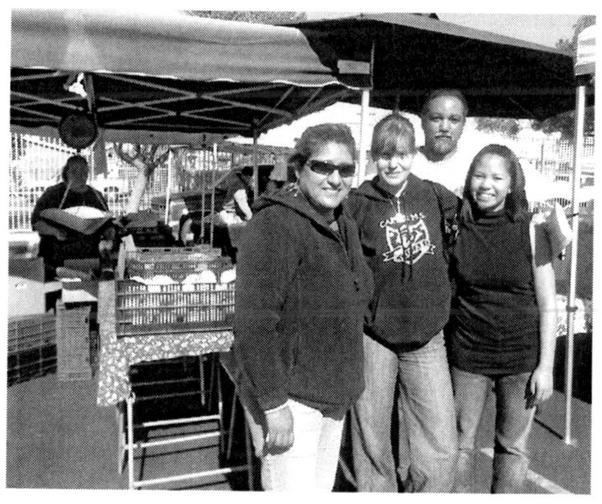

ODYSSEY OF INSPIRATION

Lorien Eck

What can I say? Where to start? My experience as a Guiding Teacher with novice arts educators for the past three has been truly remarkable and filled with great inspiration and innovation. Over 100 of my own students attending inner city schools in Los Angeles have taken direct benefit from the ArtsBridge partnerships, and the many students and adults who have been positively impacted cannot be emphasized enough. My journey with the program began in 2006 when I had first come in contact with the program and with its director, Amy Shimshon-Santo. That first year, my middle school students at John Muir Middle School had the pleasure and privilege to learn from, and create with, two gifted scholars, Leon Hong and Muskan Srivastava, from the UCLA Department of Design and Media Arts. Last year, our ArtsBridge scholar, Lauren Akazawa, contributed through her expertise and skill set in the textile arts to our school production of *The Odyssey*, where she guided the students in the creation of the costumes and an exhibition of especially designed Greek god and goddess textile designs that accompanied the theatrical performance. In addition, students from West Adams Preparatory High School participated in a visual storytelling master class series offered by photo journalist Iris Schneider. Through this experience and its processes, one of my students, Pamela Velasquez, created an amazing audio-visual personal statement that is an invaluable tool for her future creative and career path ambitions.

Not only have the classroom learning experiences been great for the students, they have also made new connections to UCLA, the Arts, and college life. For example, 60 Muir students and 35 West Adams High School students benefited from two visits to UCLA through the Design for Sharing program, where they saw exclusive concerts at Royce Hall, visited the Fowler Museum, and participated in special dance workshops offered by ArtsBridge. Another example is the academic shadowing opportunity that the students got to take part in. It comprised a visit to UCLA during the school day. They took part in a school tour where they visited a variety of classrooms within many departments, interacted with UCLA students, dialogued with UCLA professors, and got a feel for college life. It was awesome!

Through the ArtsBridge program with UCLA Arts, my students have had the opportunity to build important skills in leadership and public speaking through participation in the Annual Symposium. For the past two years, they have elected to participate, prepare their presentation of work, and rehearse for the big day. The actual event has proven to make a huge impact on their self-development as leaders in their peer group as well as share the symposium with the larger educational community. This year, I am sure, will be no different as our ArtsBridge scholar, Sarah Nuernberg, at West Adams Preparatory

High School is inspiring my design class students with her amazing lessons in alternative processes in photography.

There have been many other opportunities that the community partnership has provided over the years that have taken our work in the classroom to the next level. For instance, one of my students who showed a serious interest in graphic design applied for, and was awarded, a scholarship to the UCLA Summer Institute to study Design and Media Arts. Through this opportunity, she produced a self published magazine, which is in her portfolio as she enters her high school career. The relationships that we built, and opportunities that were shared, planted seeds that have born fruit in positive student impact.

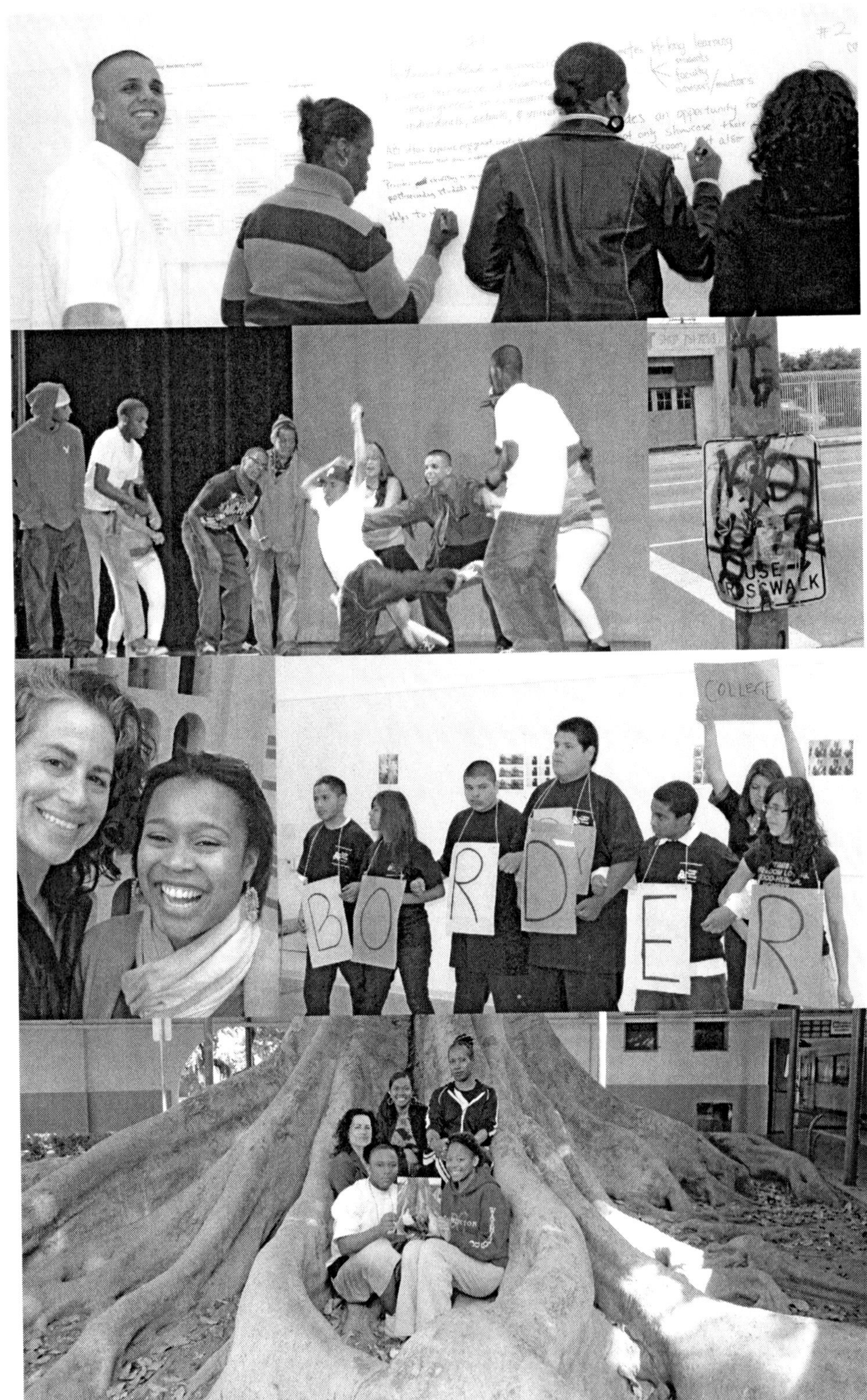

SHARING KNOWLEDGE

Assess Section Overview

Program assessment is sometimes seen as a cumbersome external requirement rather than a useful internal strategy for collective improvement. I am convinced otherwise. Feminist researchers have long argued that the social position, experience, and perspective of the researcher influence the questions one asks and the answers found.[1] In Singing Our Praises: Case Studies in the Art of Evaluation, Rory McPherson of the Wallace Foundation states that knowledge itself is crucial to social change. He writes, "Arts groups that collect, use and share the knowledge they gather not only increase their own effectiveness but also contribute to the growing understanding of the benefits of cultural participation and the unique value of the arts."[2] Assessment requires asking oneself: What do I care about? What am I doing? What can be done better, and how? Community partnerships benefit from questioning, understanding, and sharing knowledge about what is done (or not done), how, and why. In this way, the group can better understand and share the real impact group action has on participants.

Working together with an ethic of rigor, reciprocity, and mutual respect permitted a participatory process of inquiry where students and teachers could ask questions that were relevant to their lives, share learning strategies that worked, and use this knowledge to transform not only themselves, but the educational institutions that frame teaching and learning.

This section provides a range of qualitative and quantitative assessments for readers from personal testimony to critical writing, from student work to statistical analysis of personal and social change. The process of questioning and sharing is apparent at the micro-level of aesthetic valuing in the classroom, to the macro level of group gatherings and social research. Most importantly, the assessment process focused on participation. Community partners were invited into the formative process, as we developed a logic model for input and possible outcomes from participation. Focus groups included youth, teachers, university alumni, school and university administrators, district representatives, and university faculty. We worked closely with evaluation expert Mark Hansen of SRM evaluation to construct a logic model and develop online and print survey instruments for youth, teachers, and university students. Youth perspectives within the focus groups inspired a focus on personal efficacy and changing perceptions of self and others. In the words of one high school student, participation was helping students "find their true self."

Each year, every step of the way, diverse program participants shared in the inquiry process of communal action, open discussion, and annual gatherings. The geographic spread of our work, the interdisciplinary nature of arts instruction, and the vitality of annual intergenerational gatherings provided an opportunity to bridge Los Angeles's educational and economic fault lines. Honest questions about how geography, identity, inequality, and power impacted educational opportunity rose to the forefront while participants capably represented their own learning experiences and shared new ideas and strategies for arts education innovation.

This section provides different windows and ways for sharing what was learned from the participation process. At the end of each year, school site teams of youth, arts educators, guiding teachers, parents, and school administrators presented their school projects alongside UCLA students at the university. Each team would include an original research theme related to its arts education experience, key questions for teaching and learning, analysis of a few select issues, and shared evidence of learning through public exhibition or performance of student works. Two outstanding presentations of student work are shared along with select teacher observations, and a statistical analysis of surveys data from youth, teacher, and university students who participated in the program.

The first art piece Tameka Norris built after enrolling in UCLA's undergraduate program was a metal water fountain in the art building with the word "colored" scrawled above it. She used sculpture to demonstrate her outrage at being the only incoming African American art student that year. When I first met Ms. Norris, she was adamant about opening pathways to make university art studies more accessible for black and brown youth. She wanted to teach. Norris worked closely with Guiding Teacher Kori Hamilton at David Starr Jordan High School in Watts to design and teach an SAT vocabulary art residency. "Finding Meaning in College Bound Words" includes written and spoken feedback from the students in her class along with their paintings.

While navigating his first year as an undergraduate transfer student at UCLA, Luis Flores decided he would try and balance his own studies by teaching teenagers how to draw in Compton. At the time, in addition to being a full time UCLA student, Flores juggled two part time jobs – one in the service sector and another drawing for Marvel Comics. He quickly gained the admiration of his diligent students at Dominguez High

School and led them through the steps to draw realistic self-portraits they were very proud of. "'I Can Do This!': Portraying Self Through Portraiture" includes impressive student work and personal testimonies from students in his class.

"Lessons Learned" complements anecdotal and artistic analysis with formal statistical analysis. The chapter first revisits the program aims and provides a general context for understanding the program goals. It then discusses the formal participatory evaluation process and summarizes the statistical findings from two years of evaluation data.

Asking and answering questions is crucial to program assessment, but equally important is how that knowledge is shared and with whom. Gathering together each year was a valuable ritual for sharing processes and assessments, and for building community. When we gathered, middle school students could more easily imagine being in high school, and high school students were encouraged to envision themselves as future university students. University students were inspired by the classroom teachers and administrators to imagine post-graduation careers in arts education, and, likewise, to consider further graduate studies or careers in higher education as future faculty. Our intergenerational bonds of mentorship and community inspired dreamers at different phases of their lives to take their next bold steps.

Notes

1   *See Sandra Harding (1987) Feminism & Methodology, Bloomington: Indiana University Press, and Sharlene Nagy Hesse-Biber (2004) Feminist Perspectives on Social Research, New York: Oxford University Press for important discussions about feminist approaches to inquiry.*

2   *Suzanna Callahan's (2004) study Singing Our Praises: Case Studies in the Art of Evaluation, New York: Association of Performing Arts Presenters is a valuable comprehensive resource for arts evaluation.*

FINDING MEANING IN COLLEGE BOUND WORDS THROUGH VISUAL ART

Tameka Norris with Kori Hamilton

Key Questions

How does expressing personal meaning impact teaching and learning?
How can visual arts enrich language learning in SAT preparation?
How can integrated curriculum increase student satisfaction in learning?

Student and Teacher Reflections on Learning

For most of my students it was their first time painting, and it was their first time in a formal critique, and it was their first time having to talk about artwork. As an artist, I would say that making the work is the easiest part and talking about it is probably the hardest. They have completely blown me away with their honesty ... I appreciated the honesty. It provided a safe space for me to be sharing my story and sharing my experience as a first time teacher.

- TAMEKA NORRIS, ARTSBRIDGE SCHOLAR

I was excited when Tameka came because it was kill and drill for twenty weeks: fifteen words, take a test, fifteen words, take a test. Kill and drill is not very exciting for me, and is far from exciting for my students. When she came in and they started exploring the SAT vocabulary through visual arts and painting their oral language began to change because you could see that they were finding true connections to the word and the language. Their writing improved, and their academic language improved...Just her coming in with this visual accent to the vocabulary, with the same words that we have been using, the students' ability to grasp and truly connect with the words was phenomenal.

- KORI HAMILTON, GUIDING TEACHER

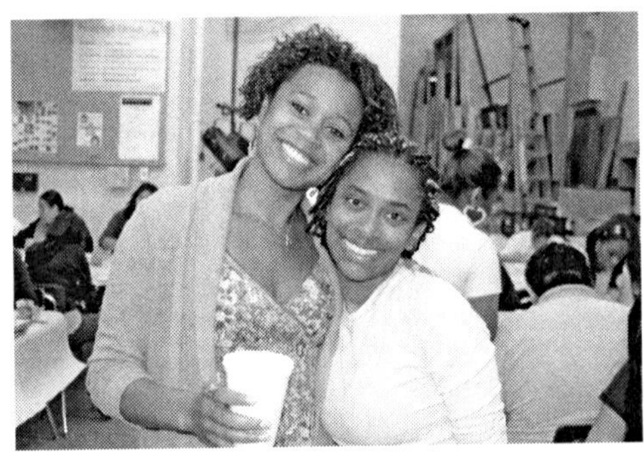

Nashale's Word

Affable [adjective] Friendly, good-natured, or easy to talk to: an affable and agreeable companion.

Zindy's Word

Abscond [verb] Leave hurriedly and secretly, typically to avoid detection of or arrest for an unlawful action such as theft: she absconded with the remaining thousand dollars.

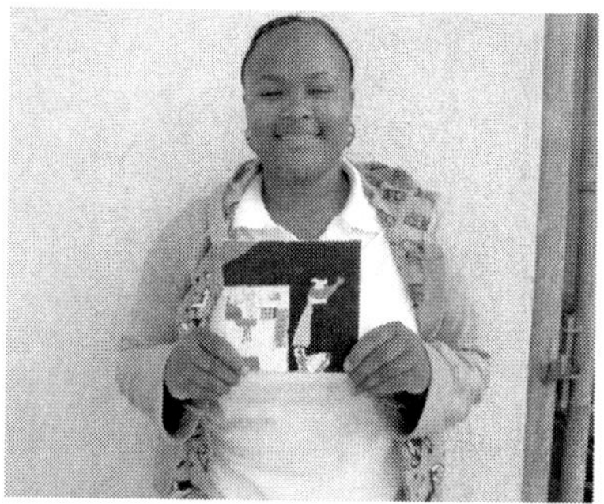

Nashale Andrews

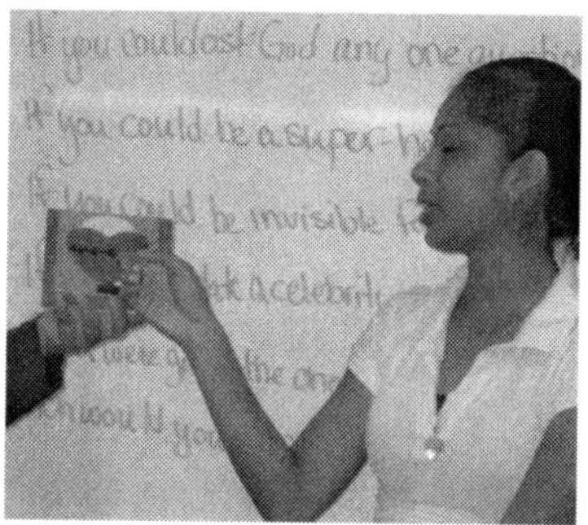

Zindy Valdovinos

In my painting I drew a heart in the middle, which represents my love for everyone who I care about even though they might not realize it because I don't really show it. The thorns across the heart represent the struggles that I have to go through daily at home, but when I'm around others I don't show it even though deep inside my heart I feel sad. The light bulb behind the heart embodies my intelligence. In the past people have told me that I don't look smart, but once they got to know me they realized that I really am smart. The blue around the light bulb and the heart represent the sky. When I look at the sky I always think positive because it's so beautiful. My entire painting shows the things that others who do not know me don't realize when they first see me.

- ZINDY VALDOVINOS

I would like to say that I enjoyed having the opportunity for expressing myself through painting, and, also, that I showed people all of the violence that occurred around me going on. We also got to learn our new SAT vocabulary word that you don't hear too often in everyday life. I kind of wished this program could have lasted longer because it's not everyday that you learn and have fun at the same time. I'm glad that I got the chance to do this.

- NASHALE ANDREWS

Edwin's Word

Aberration [noun] A departure from what is normal, usual, or expected, typically one that is unwelcome: they described the outbreak of violence in the area as an aberration.

Joana's Word

Amorous [adjective] showing, feeling, or relating to sexual desire.

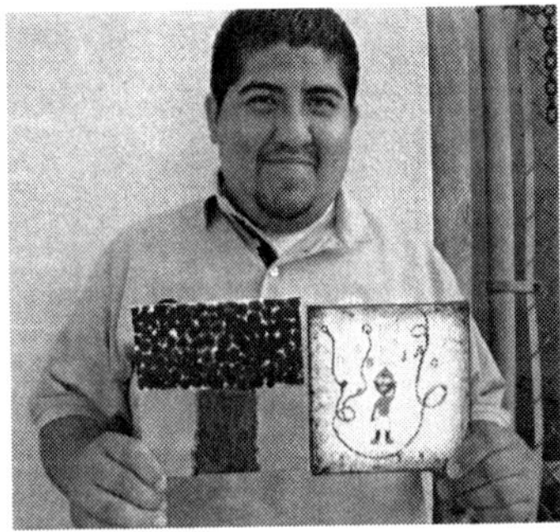

Edwin Vizcarra

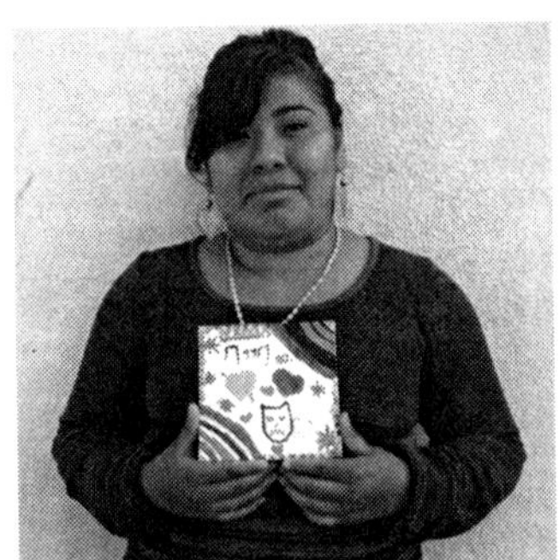

Joana Estrada

My name is Edwin...In the middle of the painting there is a turquoise dot that is being covered by other black dots. My word is aberration. It means something that is different, out of the normal, not like everyone else, basically as unique as you can get. I became inspired. The bottom half is boys that signify themselves with the color blue, girls pink, and me – being from the gay community – I just use purple because when you mix those two together that's what you get. The second piece is splattered purple because I'm just a purple bubble floating around out there, and listening to music because that's how I get away from everything.

- EDWIN VIZCARRA

My name is Joana Estrada and I just wanted to say that this was an outstanding opportunity for us because we learned a lot of new things, we learned a lot of new words, and we learned how to express ourselves and tell a little bit about us and our paintings. My painting is just about different things that describe me like music and love because I'm bisexual. I chose amorous because I'm just a very nice person.

- JOANA ESTRADA

Juan's Word

Brazen [adjective] 1 bold and without shame: he went about his illegal business with a brazen assurance | a brazen hussy! 2 chiefly poetic/literary made of brass.

Julio's Word

Ballad [noun] A poem or song narrating a story in short stanzas. Traditional ballads are typically of unknown authorship, having been passed on orally from one generation to the next as part of the folk culture, a slow sentimental or romantic song.

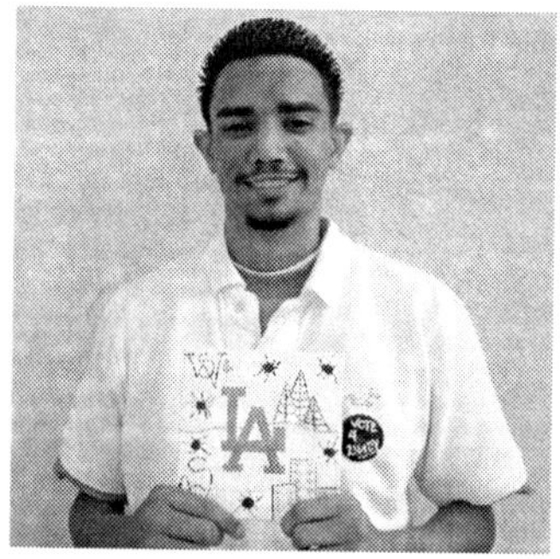

Juan Gutierrez

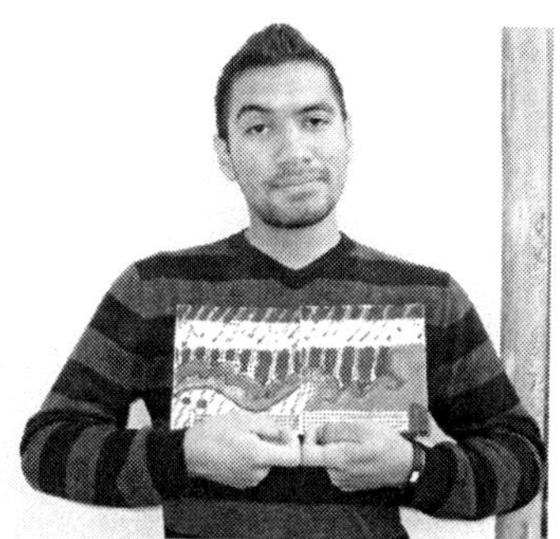

Julio Ramirez

My composition is about music. Music is a way of expressing how we truly feel about ourselves or others. In my composition I drew an instrument called a bass. My father dedicated his time to teach me how to play the bass. He also played the bass in a band at Guatemala. Going back to my composition, the fire that runs on top of the instrument represents the passion I have for music. Ever since I started playing music I couldn't stop and eventually made it part of my life. The notes that are drawn in the composition are a symbol of hard working and dedication towards music. There's always a slight fright playing on stage, but I eventually managed to overcome my fear and enjoy what I love to do. Now I play gospel music for my church and ballad is one thing I'm not afraid to express to people.

- JULIO RAMIREZ

I chose the word Brazen because it means excessively bold and brash. I think that is me, in a way. When you look at my picture you see the LA sign, you see Watts, and South Central. You might even think automatically "Watts. South Central. Bad Kid." The reason I chose those is because I am proud of where I come from. I chose brazen because I want to show everybody that even though I come from a "bad neighborhood," or whatever, that I can still pull through and make something big out of my life.

- JUAN GURIERREZ

Jesus' Word

Eclectic [adjective] 1 Deriving ideas, style, or taste from a broad and diverse range of sources: her musical tastes are eclectic.

Carina's Word

Pacific [adjective] 1 a pacific community peace-loving, peaceable, pacifist, nonviolent, nonaggressive, nonbelligerent, unwarlike. antonym aggressive, belligerent. 2 their pacific intentions conciliatory, peacemaking, placatory, propitiatory, appeasing, mollifying, mediatory, dovish; formal irenic. antonym warmongering. 3 pacific waters calm, still, smooth, tranquil, placid, waveless, unruffled, like a millpond.

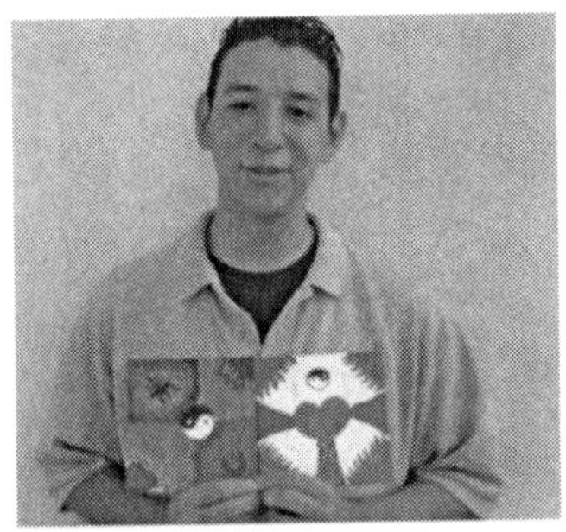

Jesus Ruiz

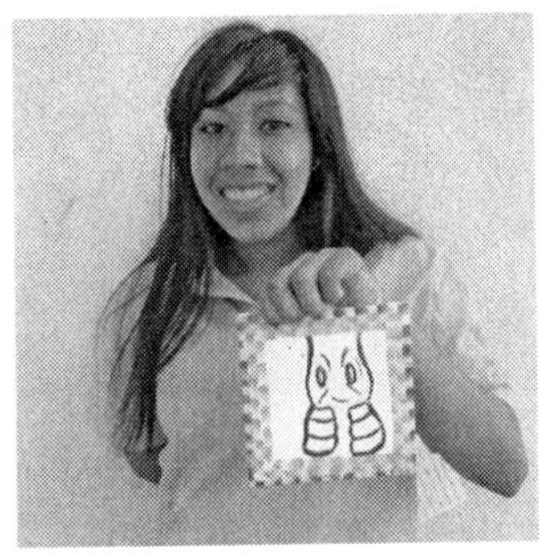

Carina Montanez

The reason I picked the word eclectic is because it means "consists of a diverse variety of elements." It is due to the fact that mine has to deal with balance of one's life. This represents me and how I am. Also, it represents how other people are as well. It shows how everyone has the burning passion of love and the burning fire of evil. Also, [it shows] how everyone has responsibility for their own life and the side they do not show to other people that is hidden. To show that I made art about balance is my center the yin-yang symbol.

- JESUS RUIZ

I rest in a magical place where all the worries fade away, where no one can bother me, and where I would like to rest. The water is pacific and the leaves of the tree are green. This is the magical place where I want to be, where the wind blows my hair softly and it wraps me like a cold blanket. I could sit here and meditate and time doesn't seem to matter, all the worries seem to fade away. Here I want to be, but in reality this place does not exist for me. Oh, how I wish I was in this pacific place.

- CARINA MONTANEZ

Antonio's Word

Unctous [adjective] 1 (of a person) excessively or ingratiatingly flattering; oily : he seemed anxious to please but not in an unctuous way. 2 (chiefly of minerals) having a greasy or soapy feel.

Maria's Word

Amalgamate [verb] Combine or unite to form one organization or structure: [trans.] he amalgamated his company with another.

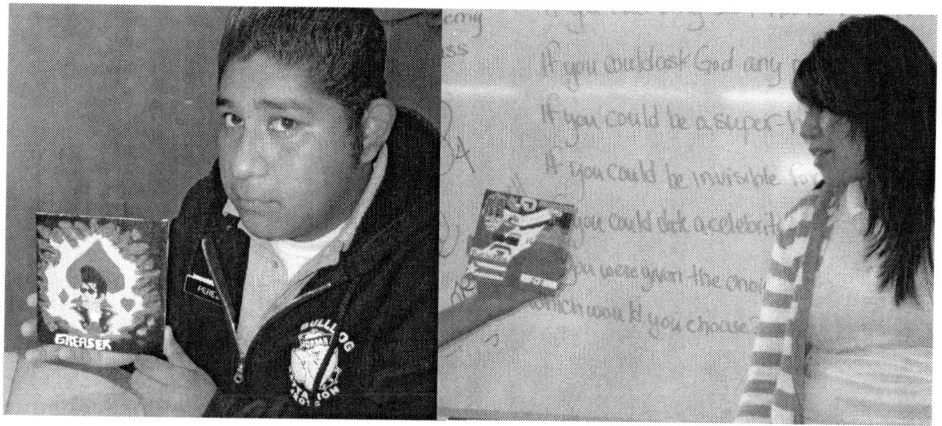

Antonio Perez   Maria Erazo

Amalgamate: to bring together. This self-portrait is another way to amalgamate my past surroundings and my present. The two flags represent my uniqueness. By them I have learned to appreciate my cultures and be proud of where I come from. The violence around our neighborhood is always unexplainable because you have no idea if the cops are to blame or the people involved. The guy lying on the floor is a symbol of what we see or hear each day. The angel represents what becomes of everyone who dies and goes onto the road to heaven.

- MARIA ERAZO

"I CAN DO THIS!"
PORTRAYING SELF THROUGH PORTRAITURE

Luis Flores with Jerry Reed

Key Questions

How does studying portraiture impact students' observation skills and ability to see themselves and their environment?

How is the motivation to learn sparked by seeing one's own image emerge from a blank page?

How can the art critique process provide a forum for sharing personal preferences, opinions, constructive criticism, and self-reflection?

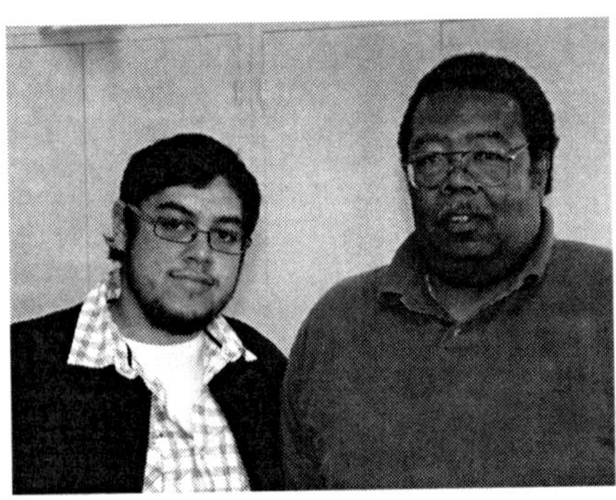

Something that I noticed about my class was that after they spent some time looking at themselves for hours and hours and hours you could tell that they got bored, and it was that boredom that they needed for them to notice these other things that they probably had overlooked before. They started to gain some confidence. They noticed that "Oh, I can do this. Oh, just [put] a little more effort and a little more time." They were able to push themselves and get the work done ... Another thing that I noticed was that after starting from nothing, putting lines on a blank paper, once they saw that "That kind of looks like my eye. That kind of looks like my mouth." It gave them the motivation they needed to push themselves even further.

— LUIS FLORES, ARTSBRIDGE SCHOLAR

I just want to thank Luis Flores and the ArtsBridge program for inviting us to participate. I have been a teacher for many many years now and it's the first time that we have been a part of a program like this and it's the first time that we have been invited to present in a forum like this. It does a lot for the students' confidence and it does a lot for the program.

— JERRY REED, GUIDING TEACHER

Student and Teacher Reflections on Learning

We are going to look at some of the slides of my students' work. It is important to note that none of my students had ever done any type of portraiture before. So, this is what they were able to do with the right motivation and their own dedication to it. I am very proud of them.

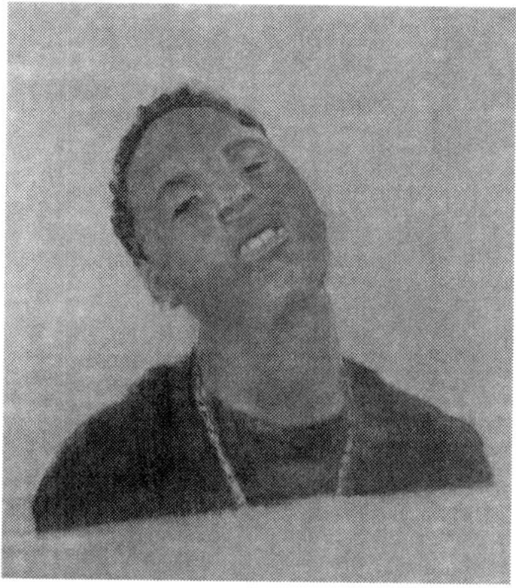

This is Javan [Polk]. What I really liked about his portrait are the highlights that he put above his cheekbones and his nose. It made it very three dimensional for me, and I just love the pose. Shalenia Mack was really nervous at first. She didn't have enough faith in herself, but after getting going, putting that pencil on paper, she was able to see that it was coming together. She actually changed her hair because from the picture she had braids. She was able to transform herself. I'm very proud of her for that. This is Timothy [Powell]. The smile on his face is so contagious that I can't help but smile. The shading with the eyes, his chin, and the mouth came out really well.

- LUIS FLORES

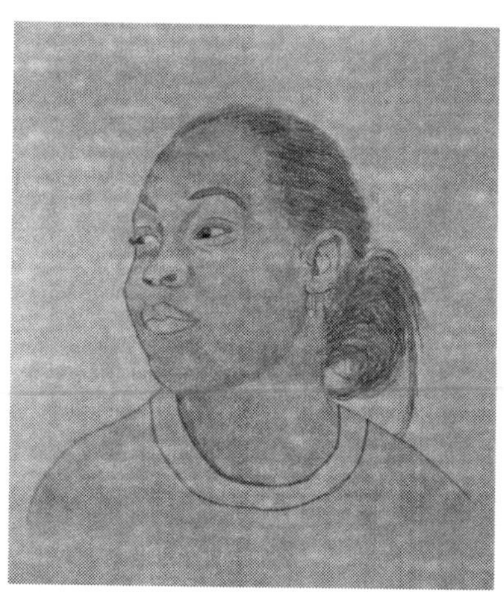

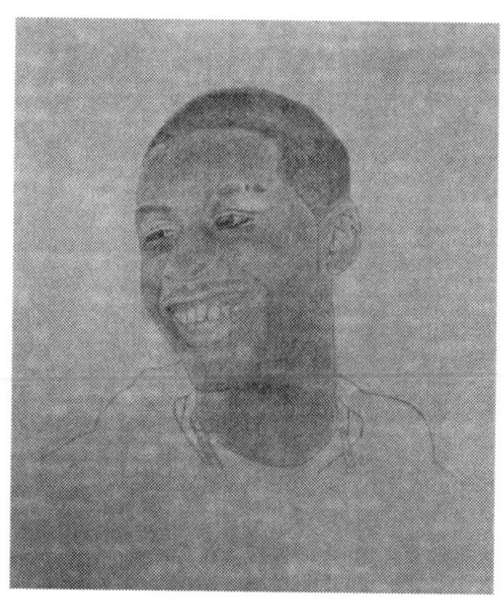

Self Portraits by Javan Polk, Shalenia Mack, and Timothy Powell

My name is Leo Perez and this is my first portrait of myself. The hard thing about it was to try and come up with a different style than the rest of the class. The shading was really difficult because I had no idea how to start it. This is what I came up with. I was surprised at the end.

- LEO PEREZ

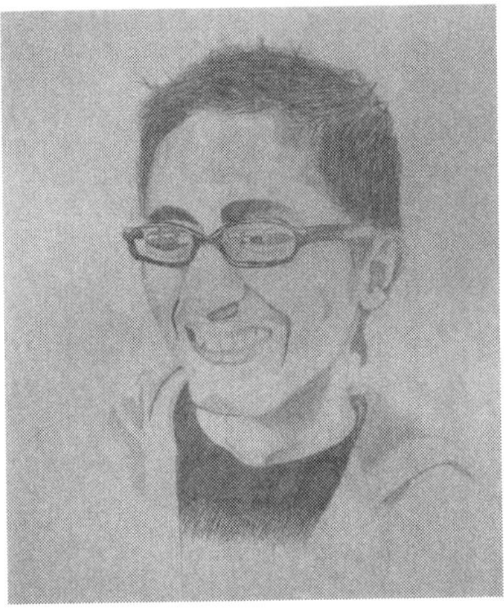

My name is Shacarra Crawford and this is my first portrait. When he [Luis] first came I didn't really think that I could do a portrait – especially of myself. It was kind of difficult for me, and Luis, he worked with me. After awhile I was like 'I can do this. I can do this.' So, it gave me great confidence and by doing this I know that I can do more self-portraits and take my drawings beyond.

- SHACARRA CRAWFORD

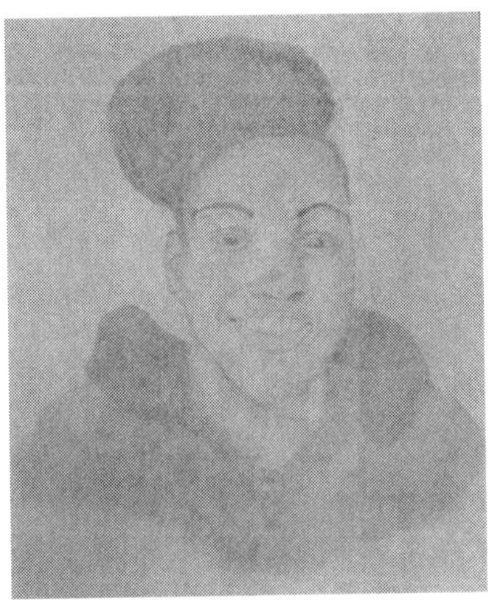

I CAN DO THIS

This is my first self-portrait that I ever drew, and also my first year in art class. I am very glad and surprised with the results. It came out really good. The only problem that I had was with the shading, just like Leo, but Luis helped me out with the shading. I had some trouble with the hair, but Luis showed me the way ... Drawing has actually given me more confidence about learning or trying new arts styles and techniques.

- ERICK PARRA

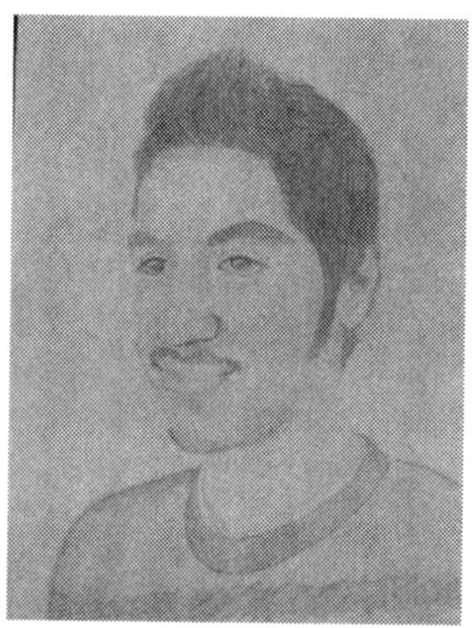

After we did the portraits we did a final critique and during the critique process it allowed the students to see what everyone else was doing. Everyone ... [had been] doing their own thing and not really sharing. In the beginning everyone was kind of shy but then we got to see everyone's work it allowed people to be proud of themselves and allowed the other students to give the respect that they deserve in terms of their work. I definitely have a new respect for teachers. It is not easy being a teacher. It is very difficult. I would like to give them credit! It's not easy trying to be an artist, getting things to work, and it's not easy trying to put a lesson together. I have also learned to stay committed ... I am so glad that I stuck it out because I would have been upset with myself for not having had this moment, and being able to see that I helped them do that. It's been great and I am so proud of my students. I have high expectations for you, and I know that you can do whatever you guys want in terms of art, or anything else.

- LUIS FLORES

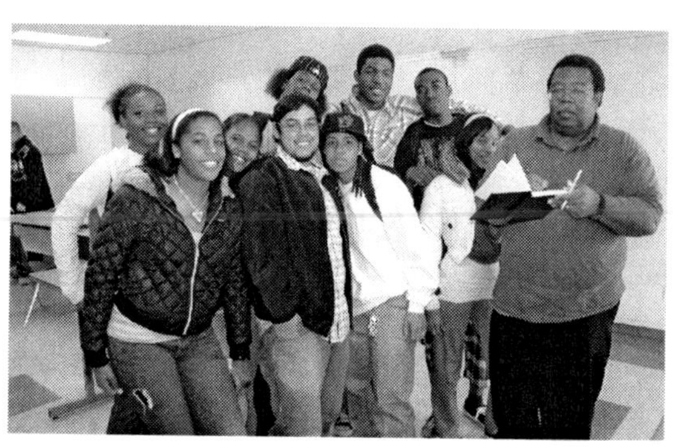

LESSONS LEARNED

Amy Shimshon-Santo

Conclusions are opportunities to reflect back and imagine forward. What have we learned along the way? Have we met our aims? This conclusion begins by revisiting and framing the program aims within the historical and geographic context of California. It also summarizes the formal evaluation process, including logic modeling, focus groups, and survey processes, and shares significant findings from analysis of pre and post participation surveys collected from university students and school aged youth. While the vivid personal stories and thoughtful social analysis in this book constitute qualitative assessments of our actions, this chapter identifies the specific quantifiable impact from participation.

While each program site is distinctive, every ArtsBridge Program in the University of California system is held accountable to statewide Student Academic Preparation and Education Partnerships (SAPEP) goals. The SAPEP mission is to

> *Raise student achievement levels generally and to close achievement gaps between groups of students throughout the K20 pipeline so that more educationally disadvantaged students are prepared for postsecondary education, to pursue graduate and professional school opportunities, and to achieve success in the workplace (University of California: 2005).*

The importance of inspiring educational attainment through the Arts cannot be underestimated. A recent study found that, despite persistent inequalities connected to gender, race, ethnicity, and foreign or native-born status, educational attainment remains directly linked to economic opportunity (Crissey 2009). Census data also shows that California is below the national mean for high school completion (Crissey 2009). Systematic obstacles appear to be disproportionately hindering educational attainment for African-American and Latino youth. In 2007, 17.3 percent of African Americans and 12.5 percent of Latinos in California completed a Bachelors degree or higher, as compared to 30.5 percent of Non-Hispanic Whites and 49.5 percent of Asians (Crissey 2009:10). Clearly, problems in K-12 public schooling are important to higher education, since colleges and universities cannot achieve excellence in diversity, teaching, research, and service without caring about the feeder system from which they draw in K-12 schools. With proper investment of time, energy, expertise, and resources, positive actions can successfully support high school graduation and college preparation and will cultivate a diverse, qualified pool of future emerging artists and faculty for higher education in the arts.

Addressing the K-20 pipeline in the Arts is crucial to the vitality and diversity of higher education, but, also, to the Los Angeles regional economy as a whole. Analysis of the *Creative Economy of the Los Angeles Region* (2008) found that creative sector jobs have been recognized as "one of the largest business sectors in the [Los Angeles] region," generating "one million direct or indirect jobs in Los Angeles and Orange Counties" (2008: 1). In addition, jobs in the creative industries are on the rise, growing 2.8% between 2002 and 2007 (2008: 23).

A systematic lack of preparation in the skills needed for youth to compete in the creative economy has social justice implications for the next generation. Obviously, it is contradictory to disinvest in K-12 arts education in a region where the creative sector is a major force driving the economy (LACEDC 2008). That, however, is the current trend. *The Unfinished Canvas* (Woodworth et. al.) found that a whopping "89% of California K-12 schools fail to offer a standards-based course of study in all four disciplines—music, visual arts, theatre, and dance—and thus fall short of state goals for Arts education (2007: 6)." In addition, "Students attending high-poverty schools have less access to arts instruction than their peers in more affluent communities (2007: 4)"

Solutions to these problems are attainable with proper attention and sustained dedication from different sectors of the "arts world," including higher education. Woodworth suggests that educational institutions "develop a long-range strategic plan for Arts education, dedicate resources and staff, and provide for the ongoing evaluation of arts programs (2007:4)." In addition, the report recommends "improv[ing] teacher professional development in Arts education...[and] consider[ing] credential reforms" (2007:4). Currently, credentials exist in Visual Arts and Music, but do not exist in the equally relevant disciplines of Theater and Dance. Historically, the task of credentialing has been forwarded to the California State University system, while research universities tended to steer clear of this issue. The question, given the magnitude of the problem, becomes how can the arts and educational sectors afford not to get involved. During my time at ArtsBridge, we were able to begin to address the credentialing issue by collaborating with the Graduate School of Education and Information Studies / Center X's Teach LA / Teach Compton program, along with the Los Angeles Unified School District's Arts Education Branch, to provide a Physical Education: Dance Emphasis credential option and hire Arts interns to teach in high needs urban schools. This action would be in alignment with the federal administration's interest in developing an urban arts corps (Obama 2009).

Formal Evaluation Process

This section shares statistically relevant program outcomes from the UCLA Arts ArtsBridge program from 2006 to 2009. This statistical summary is best seen as a complement to the rich qualitative reflections offered by youth, parents, classroom teachers and UCLA students in this book. With the capable guidance of Mark Hansen, at SRM Evaluation, we developed original logic models, convened focus groups, and refined survey tools to evaluate the program. Developing new logic models for program evaluation allowed us to outline clearly proposed connections between creative service inputs and projected short-term outputs and long terms outcomes. The logic models also allowed our program to include areas of assessment that went beyond participants' interest levels in attending college. After one Lynwood High School student named Ulysses explained in a focus group that ArtsBridge "helped students find their true self," we wanted our evaluation methods to include participants' perceptions of self and peers, community awareness, and the vision of their future.

The focus groups we convened included a diverse spectrum of participants, including youth, ArtsBridge alumni, host teachers, school principals, and district representatives. The different perspectives provided by youth and adults increased transparency, inspired momentum, and allowed the groups to include and value the perspectives of different types of stakeholders.

Finally, we developed new survey tools that allowed data input and statistical computation to be done online through SurveyMonkey as well as in a paper format. The online shift proved challenging, since our site belonged to a broader network that was not digitizing its survey tools at the time. However, while this was initially cumbersome, it was nonetheless a positive attempt to bring evaluation methods forward to meet 21st century procedures. In addition to asking some new questions and digitizing the answers, we decided to include in our site student surveys, rather than simply host teachers' or ArtsBridge Scholars' perceptions of their students, to allow young people to express their views on program participation in their own voices. Also, the emphasis on quantitative data was matched by collection of valuable and qualitative assessments through student work samples, lesson plans, journaling, and academic writing. Finally, the assessment processes, products, and perspectives were shared with the broader public through: 1) school site culminations; 2) an annual symposium at UCLA; and 3) a community-based publication.

During the first year of the previously mentioned assessment, we were able to include only post-participation information. However, by the second year, we were able to perform preliminary, mid-level, and post participation surveys of youth, scholars, and host teachers. These processes increased the viability of data collected, proved useful to program planning on the ground, and, also, satisfied SAPEP requirements. (While the data collected from host teachers was also useful to the program, this essay focuses solely on outcomes for participating K-12 youth, and UCLA student scholars.)

Year One

Vivid psycho-social impacts emerged from the 2008 data regarding self-awareness, self-esteem, and positive peer relationships among youth. Over half of the youth (55%) reported that they discovered new talents or abilities in themselves as a result of program participation. The same was also true of their vision of their peers. Fifty percent of the participants reported that they discovered new talents or abilities in their classmates as a result of program participation. Youth also reported that their views about schooling and their future life opportunities shifted substantially as a result of program participation. Importantly, 67 percent reported that through participation in ArtsBridge, they became more confident about [their] future. This finding tracks a tangible rise in self-confidence and hope. Student views about higher education also changed dramatically: 64% reported becoming more interested in going to college; 49% became more interested in a career in the arts; and 67% reported greater confidence in his/her ability to attend college.

The 2008 impact data for ArtsBridge Scholars was equally as positive as it was for the students that they were instructing. They reported that the program helped them better value their roles as artists in society and envision their own future goals. After participation, 100% of the ArtsBridge Scholars strongly agreed with the notion that artists make positive contributions to society, and all of the scholars reported that they were proud of their artistic abilities and how they were using them. Seventy two percent of participants agreed or strongly agreed that the program helped them identify future goals upon graduation.

Also interesting, 33% of the 2008 ArtsBridge Scholars indicated that UCLA had prepared them "extremely well." In comparison, when asked about their experiences with ArtsBridge, 56% indicated that their experiences had prepared them "extremely well" to pursue their future plans. This finding suggests that the scholars believe that ArtsBridge provided better, or more relevant, training or preparation for pursuing their goals than UCLA. Also important, 82% reported that through their experiences as ArtsBridge scholars, they were more likely to pursue careers as teaching artists.

Year Two

In 2009, pre and post surveys queried youth in the following three areas: academic language in the Arts; perception of self and peers; and future interest in college. Since the full range of findings cannot be properly discussed within the confines of this article, I will focus on the area of greatest statistical impact -- self-esteem and positive peer relationships.

Given the low levels of access to arts education in ArtsBridge partner schools, many youth are denied the opportunity to cultivate their areas of creativity. We wanted to find out if increased opportunities for creative expression might help students identify new avenues for self-expression and personal success. Quantitative analysis suggests an exponential rise in positive impact on self-perception, as well as opinions of classmates, as a result of program participation. The results are shown in the following table.

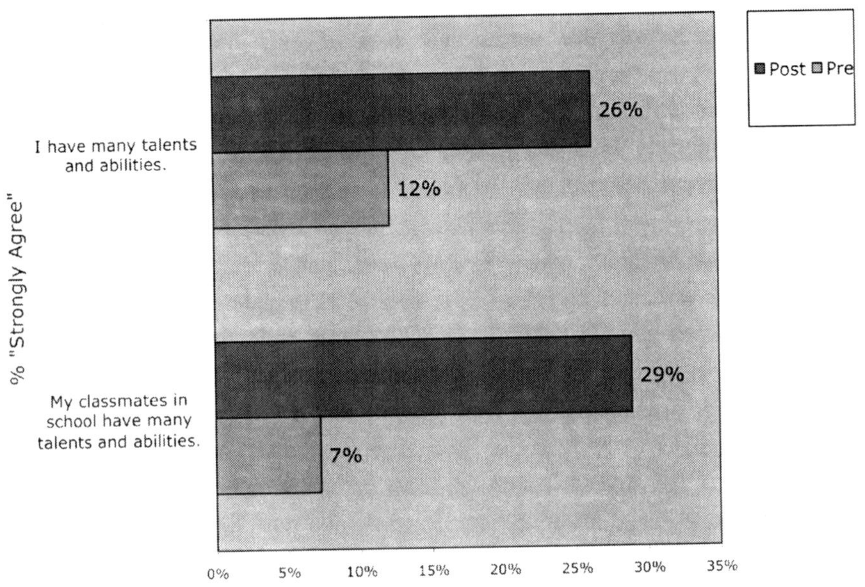

The ability to perform pre and post participation surveys provided a clearer picture of impact.

At the start of the program, only 7% of students strongly agreed with the statement, "My classmates in school have many talents and abilities." At the end of the program, 29% strongly agreed -- about four times the initial percentage. Overall agreement ("strongly agree" and "agree somewhat") also increased substantially -- from 24% to 58%. Concerning students' self-concept, 12% of students at the start of the program strongly agreed with the following statement: "I have many talents and abilities." At the end of the program, 26% strongly agreed. Overall agreement increased from 39% to 50% (Hansen and Shimshon-Santo, 2009).

With positive impact observed among youth participants, how did program participation impact the ArtsBridge Scholars? As we built capacity, and program rigor grew between 2005 and 2009, we created new courses to support teacher preparation and required a two to three quarter commitment, roughly one academic year, from the emerging Arts educators. This allowed them to meet weekly under faculty guidance and to build a teaching community with their peers. By the 2008-2009 academic year, it became clear that the program's rigor was satisfying for some and unsatisfying for others. Either way, the program provided an important experimental space for young artists to gain professional preparation, and determine whether or not they wanted to include teaching in their professional or academic profiles. This realization was a valuable lesson for an emerging artist early in his or her career.

For the scholars who enjoyed arts pedagogy, many continued on to graduate programs in Arts education at other institutions, including Harvard University, New York University, the University of California, Berkeley, or California State University credentialing programs at California State University Dominguez Hills or Long Beach campuses. Other scholars were hired directly into Los Angeles charter schools and taught visual art or dance education full time while they pursued a credential. Still others were accepted into the Teach for America Program. Other alumni took alternative paths by pursuing graduate studies in their artistic genres, which involved an educational component such as new media designs for educational games, or taught their craft in the community.

To enhance our understanding of the long-term impact of program participation on UCLA students, we surveyed ArtsBridge Alumni from 2005-2009. Alumni were asked to respond to a survey regarding their current endeavors, future plans, and to rate how participation in the program prepared them for their lives after graduation.[1] Survey results found that the majority of ArtsBridge alumni (86%) had gone on to teach Art after graduation. This included teaching in public schools and non-profit art centers. Many explained that their ArtsBridge experience prepared them for leadership to initiate new arts education programs and to teach the Arts in ways that involved a wellspring of integrated topics from new technologies to dance, college preparation to young women's empowerment, and educational outreach. Since graduating from UCLA, 47 percent of the alumni respondents had pursued further schooling, and another 47 percent planned on completing further studies in the future. Once again, they previewed the program more favorably than their overall university studies. Thirty-three percent of the alumni claimed that UCLA prepared them "extremely well" for the work they were now doing, while 67 percent rated their ArtsBridge experience as preparing them "extremely well" for their lives post graduation. Alumni identified two salient skills developed in the program as particularly important: 1) curriculum development; and 2) community participation. One respondent explained: "ArtsBridge really helped me cultivate a sense of independence toward my work; ArtsBridge engages students at a level that entails more responsibility--not only to oneself, but to their supervisors and students. I feel like it prepared me to teach in any environment in California, if not the U.S., and I'm very grateful for that experience."

Quantitative and qualitative data collected from youth and scholars demonstrate significant professional, personal, and academic, impact from participation. For youth, the findings suggest that program participation was a positive tool for developing personal and social value among students in under-resourced neighborhoods. For UCLA students, program participation was ranked more valuable than for their overall general education, provided real world experience that they found useful post graduation, and helped them clarify their future goals.

Final Thoughts

This chapter began by discussing the State of California's college preparedness goals as elaborated through SAPEP, and continued on to explain how ArtsBridge programs in the University of California system are held accountable to SAPEP goals. I then briefly overviewed recent relevant research regarding the way that educational attainment relates to poverty in California; the importance of the creative economy in Los Angeles; and the failure of California to reach federally mandated goals in arts education -- particularly for under-resourced neighborhoods. Finally, I analyzed program outcomes for K-12 youth and university student participants.

The eclectic stories, qualitative analysis, and quantitative research in this book suggest important roles for higher education in arts educator preparation and in community partnerships with under-resourced schools. Data elucidates a positive impact from program participation for both K-12 students in high-needs schools and university arts students at UCLA. The findings demonstrate that participation supported educational attainment, as well as increased satisfaction with education for primary, secondary and university students.

Substantive improvements were also found in perception of self and peers, as well as self-efficacy. In her study, *Rock My Soul: Black People and Self Esteem*, bell hooks discusses the historical roots of negative perceptions of self and peers and defends the importance of building positive self esteem for personal and social uplift. She writes, " [The] combination of care, commitment, knowledge, responsibility, respect, and trust... [are] the tools we need to build healthy self-esteem" (2003: 213). This suggests that the positive impact on self esteem found through ArtsBridge may be due not only to the creative impulse of artistic practice itself, but, also, to the program's success in cultivating ongoing, reliable, caring relationships among individuals and groups in high needs learning communities and the university.

While there is growing recognition of the general importance of creativity in education (Robinson 2001), this analysis finds that creative pedagogy can also support broader social justice aims when linked to long-term community partnerships that connect K-12 schools and universities in what is being called the K-20 pipeline. In order to promote personal and social uplift, all students, regardless of the neighborhoods in which they are raised or the schools they attend, deserve the opportunity to identify and cultivate the creative skills required for participation in higher education and in today's innovative, creative economy. The lack of arts education opportunities for California youth requires broad based systematic efforts to increase access to youth and to prepare future Arts educators. Higher education, in general, and departments and schools of education and the arts, in particular, are uniquely positioned to collaborate and prepare a new generation of artists, educators, leaders, and activists who understand how creativity feeds into educational reform and social change.

Note

1   *Fifteen alumni responded to the survey. Of the respondents, 20% participated during 2007-2008, 40% during 2006-2007, 33% during 2005-2006 and 13% during 2004-2005 academic years. While at UCLA, 57% of the respondents were World Arts and Cultures majors, 36% were Art majors, 7% were Design\Media Arts majors, and 7% were Music majors. 93% of the group participated in ArtsBridge as undergraduate students.*

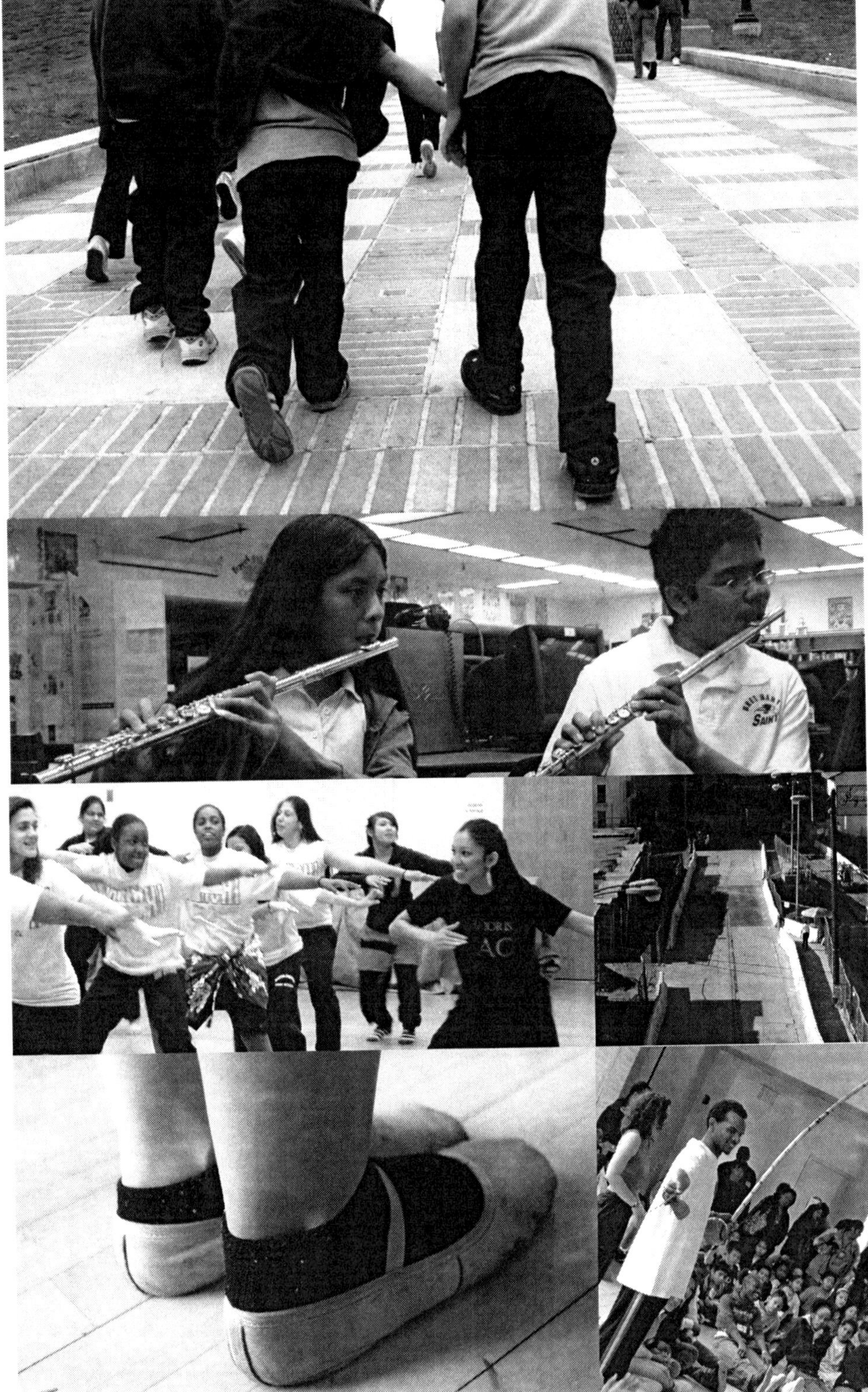

LESSON PLAN GUIDE

Concept / Focus

Summarize in no more than a few sentences the exact workshop focus, or "big idea."

Learning Outcomes

Briefly describe the specific projected learning outcomes for your students from participation. What will they understand or be able to do as a result of participating in this specific session? Your writing about learning outcomes may begin with words, such as "Students will be able to," or "Students will understand how."

Vocabulary

List new academic or creative vocabulary that will be instructed during the class. Academic vocabulary can share core concepts, ideas, or practices that are relevant to the art form you are instructing and standards of the subject area you are teaching.

VAPA Strands and Standards

School based instruction in the Arts is required to follow the Visual and Performing Arts framework and standards for instruction in your state. Arts educators can easily familiarize themselves with the strands (Artistic Perception, Creative Perception, Historical and Cultural Context, Aesthetic Valuing, Connection, Relationship, and Applications), and the specific grade level discipline standards in the art form. The state standards are posted online through your Department of Education. In California, the following resources are also recommended:

Visual and Performing Arts Framework for California Public School, Prekindergarten Through Grade Twelve, Sacramento: California Department of Education, 2004. (ISBN 0-8011-1592-2)

Visual and Performing Arts Content Standards for California Public School, Prekindergarten Through Grade Twelve, Ed O'Malley (ed.), Sacramento: California Department of Education, 2001. (ISBN 0-8011-1548-5)

Additional Relevant Standards

Integrated arts instruction combines the standards and processes for more than one discipline. Educators who teach integrated arts instruction will also include the standards addressed from other artistic or academic discipline. For example, an integrated class in visual art and science, or dance and health, or architecture and history, will include the grade levels standards addresses in both areas. All content area standards in every subject are available online through the California Department of Education at http://www.cde.ca.gov/be/st/ss/.

Materials/Technology

Include a short list of the materials you will be using in the lesson, and technological and/or spatial requirements for instruction.

Sequence of Instruction

Make a list that maps out the flow of your class and includes the time you will allot to each activity in relation to your entire instructional time. The flow of your session establishes a ritual or rhythm for instruction that your students will welcome. Seasoned teachers know that providing a balanced sequence of instruction, with clear expectations and rituals for your students, will allow you to focus more on teaching and less on classroom management.

The elements in the sequence of instruction will differ depending on your artistic discipline, and your own style, but often echo the frameworks addressed in your lesson. Common elements in a sequence of instruction include an opening ritual or activity of some kind, introduction of the class topic or "big idea" of the day, a skill building activity to practice new knowledge, a problem solving activity to put that new knowledge or skill into action through creation, a reflection or assessment activity, and a concluding ritual of some kind that might provide a brief summary review of the day and expectations for the upcoming session.

Differentiated Learning Strategies

Educators can plan special strategies for working with students that confront unique developmental issues and require alternative interventions or special attention. These teaching strategies maybe included in the lesson plan itself.

SCAFFOLDING GUIDE

General Topic of Study

Articulate the focus of a scaffolded, or conscientiously sequenced series of lessons. Summarize the larger focus of study in a few sentences including the general topic of instruction and the different subtopics, or units, that will be included.

Learning Outcomes

Outline the general projected learning outcomes for your students. What will they understand, or be able to do, as a result of participating in this sequence of units and lessons? Like in an individual lesson, your writing about learning outcomes can begin with words such as "Students will be able to..." or "Students will understand how to..." However, the learning outcomes should be broad enough to capture the sequence of lessons or units.

Vocabulary

List the overarching academic and creative vocabulary that will be instructed during the sequence of lessons. A separate handout can be made to include all of the core vocabulary. Academic vocabulary should be relevant to the art form you are instructing and reflect the standards of the subject area.

VAPA Strands and Standards

School based instruction in the Arts is required to follow the Visual and Performing Arts framework and standards for instruction in your state. Arts educators can easily familiarize themselves with the strands (Artistic Perception, Creative Perception, Historical and Cultural Context, Aesthetic Valuing, Connection, Relationship, and Applications), and the specific grade level discipline standards in the art form. The state standards are posted online through your Department of Education. In California, the following resources are also recommended:

Visual and Performing Arts Framework for California Public School, Prekindergarten Through Grade Twelve, Sacramento: California Department of Education, 2004. (ISBN 0-8011-1592-2)

Visual and Performing Arts Content Standards for California Public School, Prekindergarten Through Grade Twelve, E. O'Malley (Ed.), Sacramento: California Department of Education, 2001. (ISBN 0-8011-1548-5)

Additional Relevant Standards

Integrated arts instruction combines the standards and processes for more than one discipline. Educators who teach integrated arts instruction will also include the standards addressed from other artistic or academic disciplines. For example, integrated classes in visual art and science, dance and health, or architecture and history, will include the grade levels standards addresses in both areas. All content area standards in every subject are available online through the California Department of Education at http://www.cde.ca.gov/be/st/ss/.

Materials/Technology

List all materials you will be require for the sequence of lessons, including technology, space, and supplies.

Scaffolding of Instruction

Map out the sequence of individual lessons and units to be taught. What would you like your students to know, or be able to do, by the end of your sequence of lessons? Begin with your final goals for student learning and think backwards, step-by-step, beginning with your final goals until you reach your first class session. What skills will they need to know first to achieve the final projected learning outcomes? What beginning skills should they learn to master first, before they will be able to develop intermediate and advanced skills?

A unit is a series of lessons on one general topic. Your scaffolding may include various units, each with its own sequence of lessons within the unit. Decide approximately how many sessions, and how much time, would be required for reaching your goals for each individual lesson, each unit, and any culminating activity. A culminating activity can be as simple as a special ritual activity in class, or as complex as a public performance or exhibition of work.

The scaffolded sequence of lessons will serve as your general road map for instruction. You will want to adapt your sequential plan as you progress, keeping in mind the rate at which your students actually learn, and other real life obstacles or advancements. Be flexible enough to adapt your projected sequence of lessons while while remaining on track with your overarching student learning aims.

SCAFFOLDING GUIDE

Example outline of sequence of lessons

General Topic: __________________

Unit 1:	Sub-Topic (Aspect of General Topic)
Lesson 1	Introduction to sub-topic
Lesson 2 – 4	Practice gaining expertise in sub-topic
Lesson 5	Problem solving and reflecting on engagement with sub-topic

Unit 2:	Sub-Topic (Aspect of General Topic)
Lesson 1	Introduction to sub-topic
Lesson 2 – 4	Practice gaining expertise in sub-topic
Lesson 5	Problem solving and reflecting on engagement with sub-topic

Unit 3:	Sub-Topic (Aspect of General Topic)
Lesson 1	Introduction to sub-topic
Lesson 2 – 4	Practice gaining expertise in sub-topic
Lesson 5	Problem solving and reflecting on engagement with sub-topic

Culmination	General Goal
Lessons 1-3	Ritual, performance rehearsal, or exhibition preparation
Lesson 4	Culminating activity (Ritual, performance, exhibition, group sharing)
Lesson 5	Personal and group reflection on student learning (General Theme, Sub Topics, and Culminating Activity). Make time for everyone to hear from each other, and create closure through a final ritual activity.

PRE & POST VOCABULARY TEST

Arts Vocabulary Assessment

Student Name ____

Class ____

Teacher ____

Date ____

Instructions: Read the word below and circle the correct definition.

Example

1)   Perspective
       a. Point of view
       b. Angle
       c. Both a and b

2)
       a.
       b.
       c.

3)
       a.
       b.
       c.

Note to Arts Educators

Make a list of approximately 10 - 15 key vocabulary words relevant to the subject you will teach your students. On the first and last day of instruction, ask your students to complete the vocabulary test. Let them know that they are not expected to know the meaning of the words in advance, but, that after you complete the series of lessons, they will be able to see how much they learned. Calculate and compare the percent correct before and after the series of lessons. Share your findings with your students and colleagues so they will be proud of their learning. This is one small way to capture the impact of your teaching on their understanding of academic language in the art form.

REFERENCES

Azzi, M. S., and Collier, S. (2000). *Le grand tango: The life and music of Astor Piazzolla.* New York: Oxford University Press.

Boal, A. (1999). *Games for actors and non-actors.* New York: Routledge.

Bourdieu, P. (1984). *Distinction:A social critique of the judgement of taste,* London: Routledge.

California Department of Education. (2004). *Visual and performing arts framework for California public school, prekindergarten through grade twelve,* Sacramento: California Department of Education.

California Department of Education. (2001). *Visual and performing arts content standards for California public school, prekindergarten through grade twelve,* E. O'Malley (Ed.), Sacramento: California Department of Education.

Callahan, S. (2004). *Singing our praises: Case studies in the art of evaluation,* New York: Association of Performing Arts Presenters.

Crissey, S. (2009). *Educational Attainment in the United States: 2007,* United States Department of Commerce, United States Census Bureau.

Dewey, J. *Experience and education.* (1938). New York: Touchstone.

Drewnowski, A., Rehm, C. D., Solet, D. (2007). Disparities in obesity rates: Analysis by zip code area. *Social Science and Medicine,* 65 (12), 1-6.

DuBois, W.E.B. (1903) *The souls of black folk,* Chicago: A.C. McClurg & Co.

Duncan-Andrade, J. M., Morrell, E. (2008). *The art of critical pedagogy: Possibilities for moving from theory to practice in urban schools.* New York: Lang Publications.

Freire, P. (1970). *Pedagogy of the oppressed.* New York: Continuum Publishing.

Gardner, H. (1999). *Intelligence reframed.* New York: Basic Books.

Harding, S. (1987). *Feminism & methodology,* Bloomington: Indiana University Press.

Hennessy-Fiske, M. (2008). Panel OKs one-year ban on new fast-food restaurants in South L.A., *Los Angeles Times*. Retrieved from http://articles.latimes.com/2008/jul/23/local/me-fastfood23

hooks, b. (2003). *Rock my soul: black people and self esteem.* New York: Washington Square Press.

Jones, N. (2002). I can. *God's son.* Sony Music.

Kellner, D. (2003). Toward a critical theory of education, *Democracy & Nature*, 1469-3720, Vol 9 (1): 51 – 64

Kremer, J. D., Moccio, K.A., Hammell, J. (2009). *Severing a lifeline: The neglect of citizen children in America's immigration enforcement policy*, Dorsey & Whitney LLP, Minneapolis, MN: The Urban Institute.

Kumanyika, S., Grier, S. (2006). Targeting interventions for ethnic minority and low-income populations, *Future Child.* Spring 16 (1):187-207.

Ladson-Billings, G., William T. W. (1995). Toward a critical race theory of education. *Teachers College Record*, 97 (1), 47-68.

National Cancer Institute. (2004). Nutrition: A new frontier in cancer research, *Cancer Bulletin*, October 19, 2004. Retrieved from http://www.cancer.gov/cam/news_stories.html

Nagy Hesse-Biber, S. (2004). *Feminist perspectives on social research*, New Work: Oxford University Press.

Neison, J., Huston, T., Goeldner J., Moon C. (2003). *Background paper on the prevention and treatment of overweight and obesity*, Kaiser Permanente, Retrieved from http://www.kpinstituteforhealthpolicy.org/kpihp/CMS/Files/Childhood_Obesity.pdf

Noguera, P. (2003). *City schools and the American dream: Reclaiming the promise of public education.* New York: Teachers College Press.

Partnership To Fight Chronic Disease. (2008). *Fighting chronic disease: The commonsense solution for comprehensive health reform.* Retrieved from http://www.fightchronicdisease.org/pdfs/FightingChronicDiseasefactsheet81009.pdf

Piazzolla, A. (1990). *Libertangos: 22 compositions 1974-79.* Darmstadt: Tropical Music.

REFERENCES

Remer, J. (1996). *Beyond enrichment: building effective arts partnerships with schools and your community*. New York: American Council for the Arts.

Tatum, B. D. (2003) *Why are all the black kids sitting together in the cafeteria?: And other conversations about race.* New York: Basic Books.

Trust for America's Health. (2009). *F as in Fat: How Obesity Polices are Failing in America.* Retrieved from http://healthyamericans.org/reports/obesity2009/

Los Angeles County Economic Development Corporation. (2008, 2009). *Otis College of Design report on the creative economy of the Los Angeles region.* Los Angeles: L. A. County Economic Development Corporation.

Obama for America. (2009). *Barack Obama and Joe Biden: Champions for arts and culture,* Retrieved from http://www.barackobama.com/pdf/issues/additional/Obama FactSheet_Arts.pdf

Rabkin, N., Redmond R. (2004). *Putting the arts in the picture: Reframing education in the 21st century.* Chicago: Columbia College.

Robinson, K. (2001). *Out of our minds: Learning to be creative.* Oxford: Capstone Publishing.

Shimshon-Santo, A. (2010). Arts impact: Lessons from ArtsBridge. *Journal for Learning through the Arts,*6(1). Retrieved from: http://escholarship.org/uc/item/8jc1p385.

______. (2009). *ArtsBridge program annual report,* N.P., Los Angeles: University of California.

Stevenson, L. M., Deasy, R.J. (2005). *ThirdSpace:When learning matters,* Washington D.C.: Arts Education Partnership.

Story, M., Kaphingst, K. M., Simone F. (2006). The role of schools in obesity prevention, *Childhood Obesity,* Princeton: The Future of Children, Spring, Vol 16 (1). Retrieved from *http://weblamp.princeton.edu/chw/briefs/AA%20schools_12.14.06_FINAL.pdf*

Weiss, C., Lichtenstien, A. L., Booth, E. (2008). *AIMprint: New relationships in the arts and learning.* Chicago: Columbia College.

Woodworth, K. R., Gallagher, H. A., Guha, R., Campbell, A. Z., Lopez-Torkos, A. M., and Kim, D. (2007). An unfinished canvas. Arts education in California: Taking stock of policies and practices. Summary Report. Menlo Park, CA: SRI International.

CONTRIBUTORS

Mehvish Arifeen was born and raised in Lahore, Pakistan. She is an accomplished singer and completed her undergraduate studies at UCLA in Ethnomusicology and International Development Studies. In 2009, Arifeen studied abroad in South Africa at the University of Capetown. She is returning to Pakistan to work in non-profit sector efforts to improve educational opportunity for women and girls.

Nashale Andrews is a sophomore at Cal State University, Northridge. She graduated from David Starr Jordan High School in 2009.

Norlyn Asprec participated in ArtsBridge in 2007 and developed a dance and nutrition curriculum to address the public health issue of childhood obesity. She was a Senate Fellow in Senator DeSaulnier's office at the State Capitol. She is currently pursuing an MA in Creative Arts Therapy with a specialization in Dance/Movement Therapy at Drexel University. She plans to continue using dance as a form of alternative medicine to treat cancer as well as other chronic diseases.

Pamela Velasquez Avila graduated from West Adams Prep High School in 2009 and is currently an Art major and full time student at Pasadena City College. She dedicates her life to the Arts and to encouraging students to participate in any form of liberal arts. Velasquez is an intern at Ryman Arts where she is a conservator and helps high school Art students who participate in Ryman art classes at USC.

Leah Bass-Baylis is Principal of a new LAUSD arts integration elementary school, Valley Region Elementary School #12. Previously, she served as Principal of the Charter High School of the Arts. While Assistant Principal at Robert A. Millikan Middle School and Performing Arts Magnet, she collaborated in the development of the ArtsBridge program at Millikan. Baylis held the position of Dance Coordinator, and eventually Dance Specialist, for the Los Angeles Unified School District. She was a contributor to the State of California dance standards and holds a Bachelor of Arts degree from Spelman College, a Master of Arts from Teacher College, Columbia University, and a Master of Science degree from Pepperdine University. Prior to her career in education, Ms. Bass-Baylis enjoyed a successful career as a dancer/ singer/ actress and choreographer performing on Broadway and in venues throughout the world.

Tomás J. Benitez has been working in the Arts and culture for forty years and has lectured on Chicano Arts and culture nationally and internationally, including Europe, Africa, Israel and Mexico. He is an advocate of Arts-based community building and continues to consult with non-profit cultural organizations to sustain funding, projects, Arts education and programming.

Laurel Bybee is a designer at the Getty Center in Los Angeles. She completed a BA in design at UCLA's Department of Design | Media Arts.

Amy Chen was an ArtsBridge Scholar during the 2008-2009 academic year when she taught art to second and third graders at Jefferson Elementary School in Compton. Chen graduated from UCLA with a BA in Fine Arts. She hopes to work as an animator or concept artist in the Entertainment industry in the future.

Lórien Eck, M. Ed, NBCT, is a dedicated and passionate Arts educator whose students enjoyed a hugely successful three year relationship with ArtsBridge. She is currently creating art, creating art education media, and teaching art in both classrooms and through the TV waves.

Tanitra Flenaugh is a doctoral candidate in Music at UCLA. Her research as an ArtsBridge Scholar on culturally relevant chamber music for middle school students became the foundation of her dissertation work.

Luis Flores is a fine artist and illustrator. He completed his BA in Art at UCLA, and is currently pursuing his teaching credential in Art at the California State University, Long Beach.

Kori Hamilton is a Ph.D. student in the Educational Leadership and Policy Studies Program at Arizona State University. She taught secondary English in Watts, CA for five years. Her interests lie in educational access and equity, Art education and generally in helping children of color to be their own advocates of education.

Shannon Hickey received her BA in Art from UCLA where she was an ArtsBridge Scholar during 2008-2009. She taught second and third grade students English Language Development skills in conjunction with color theory. She is now a graduate student in the Teacher Education Program at UCLA's Graduate School of Education and Informational Studies. She hopes to become a creative and innovative arts elementary school teacher in the future.

The seeds of Ji-Ling Lin's interest in arts education was planted in 2006 when she taught photography to middle school students as an ArtsBridge Scholar. The seed is now blossoming, and Lin leads nature arts education in the woods with both children and adults through photo, dance, music, and theater.

Lindsay Lindberg was a dance educator and ArtsBridge Scholar for three years while pursuing her BA at UCLA in World Arts and Cultures with a dance emphasis. She is now a graduate student in Arts Education at New York University.

Marina Osthoff Magalhães is a Brazilian-born choreographer, performer, and arts educator who completed her undergraduate studies at UCLA with the support of an International Moss

Scholarship. She participated in ArtsBridge and graduated with a BA in World Arts and Cultures with a Dance Concentration and a minor in Women's Studies. She is a member of the LA-based Urban Latin Dance Theater company, CONTRA-TIEMPO, and looks forward to creating her own artistic work, pursuing an MFA in choreography, and further developing her skills and experience as a teaching artist.

Ellen Mulvanny received her M. Arch from UCLA's Department of Architecture and Urban Design in 2010 and holds a B.A. from Harvard University in the History of Art and Architecture. She continues to preach, practice and pursue creative problem solving through design.

Tameka Norris recently graduated from UCLA and will be attending Yale University in 2010. At Yale, she will pursue an MFA with a concentration in painting. Her future includes making art, teaching as a professor, and curating. Originally from the Mississippi Gulf Coast, Norris is also focusing on issues regarding Hurricane Katrina and, most recently, the Gulf oil spill.

Sarah G. Nuernberger fell in love with photography at a young age because of its ability to convey emotion and touch individuals from all backgrounds. She attended UCLA majoring in Art, where she was an ArtsBridge Scholar. After graduating from UCLA, she started teaching Art full time. The knowledge and experience she gained from ArtsBridge was invaluable to her as she became a middle school and high school Art teacher.

Lisa Nuñez has been a student of the arts her entire life. Since 2001, she has incorporated the arts into her Social Studies classes at Millikan Middle School Performing Arts Magnet and was thrilled to welcome ArtsBridge into her class.

Alicia Paniagua came to the United States from El Salvador. She is as an instructional assistant for the Rialto Unified School District and is pursuing an MBA from Grand Canyon University. One of her fondest memories from her undergraduate experience at UCLA came from her involvement in the ArtsBridge Program. She takes pride in the many lives that were impacted by teaching "Salsa Through the Americas."

Iliana Phirippidis was a UCLA ArtsBridge Scholar in 2007, where she integrated Theater Arts into a high school English classroom in Los Angeles. She is currently working as a fourth and fifth grade teaching assistant at North Oakland Community Charter School in Oakland, CA while she is pursuing a teaching credential through the Bay Area Teacher Training Institute.

Jerry Reed taught Art at Dominguez High School in Compton for twenty years and was the Visual and Performing Arts (VAPA) Chairperson for ten years. He received a BA in Art from Pomona College in 1971 and an MA in Education in 1980. Reed retired in 2009.

Iris Schneider has worked for the *New York Times*, the *Philadelphia Inquirer*, *Rolling Stone* and the *Los Angeles Times*. She traveled the world for the *Los Angeles Times*, covering everything from the Cannes Film Festival to poverty in Appalachia and the war in El Salvador. After working at the *Times* for 27 years photographing, writing and photo editing feature sections, she left the paper in 2007 to resume her career as a freelance photographer and writer.

Zindy Valdovinos will begin her sophomore year at UCLA in the fall. She decided school was important while growing up in Watts, because she noticed it was the only way to make it out and be somebody one day. She did not want to end up either a high school drop out, pregnant, gang affiliated, or dependent on the government for economic support. Yet, the community she grew up in made her who she is today. ArtsBridge impacted her education by helping her build social skills with others and improve her reading skills with Art.

Edwin Vizcarra is 19 years of age and is a part of the gay community. Being a part of ArtsBridge helped him express himself through art. Vizcarra graduated from Jordan High School and now works there with the EDUCARE After School Foundation as a site coordinator. He is striving to be a graphic designer.

Cynthia Wennstrom's decision to teach art was grounded in the desire to work with youth and help them make sense of their experiences in the world. Her own art practice has been about mashing up the cultural narratives people internalize as youth and investigating the tensions created as they grow and learn more about the world. Art informs her teaching, and teaching informs her art; both are always shifting, expanding, and merging with each other. She continues to make art in New York City in addition to pursuing a Master's degree in Art Education at New York University.

About the Editor

Dr. Amy Shimshon-Santo is an artist and educator who believes that creativity is pivotal to personal growth and community development. As the instigator of this volume, she facilitated the community partnerships, developed the coursework, and mentored the arts educators who share their experiences in *Arts = Education*. Her belief in the power of memory motivated her to compile, edit, and design this work so that participants' stories could be shared. Before directing the ArtsBridge Program at UCLA's School of the Arts and Architecture, she enjoyed a rewarding career in dance, performing and teaching throughout the United States and abroad at venues including the John F. Kennedy Center. She was an arts educator in Los Angeles with the Music Center Education Division for twenty years, and was a professor at UCLA for seven years. Her efforts at UCLA lay the foundation for the first Physical Education: Dance Emphasis credential in the State of California and the first undergraduate minor in Arts Education offered the University of California. She has extensive non-profit management experience in production, program start-ups, and community based initiatives. Her international work includes co-directing a transnational performing ensemble (Brazil/United States) for fifteen years, collaborations with the VIVA! Project, and outreach campaigns for the Art Center / United Nations (UNFPA and UNIFEM). She is recipient of the Presidential Honor Roll for Service Learning, a commendation from the State of California, and fellowships from the CORO Foundation, the California Arts Council, the University of California, and the Dana Foundation.

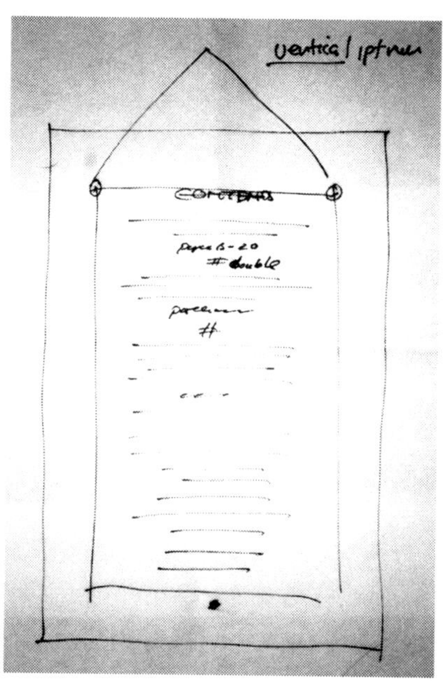
vertical / iptrver
CONTENTS
pages 16-20
double
preliminary
#

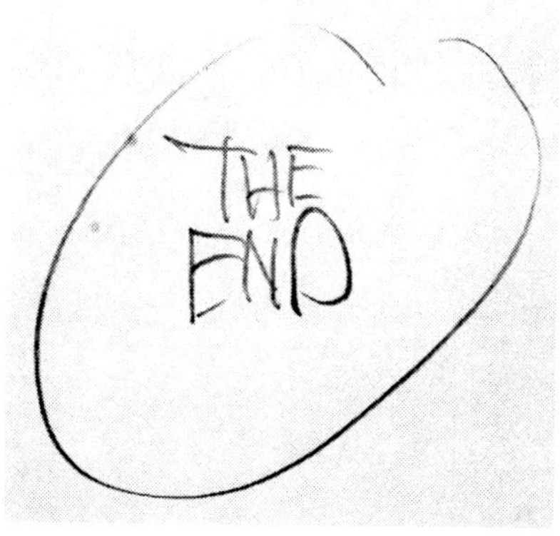
THE
END